A REVELATION OF WEALTH

Discovering Your 12 Streams of Income and Fulfillment

By
Jack Harris

A Revelation of Wealth

Discovering Your 12 Streams of Income and Fulfillment

© 2021, Jack Harris.

Print ISBN: 978-1-098387-242
eBook ISBN: 978-1-09838-7-259

Before starting this book, take a moment and consider where you want your life to lead you. What does wealth and fulfillment look like to you right now? Why do you feel you haven't discovered your potential?

_____

_____

_____

_____

_____

_____

_____

_____

_____

Once you finish, cross out the above answer. Close your eyes, breathe deeply, and tell yourself it is time to open yourself to new possibilities.

Now, turn the page.

INTRODUCTION

I remember clearly one particular night, many years back, when I was in an incredibly low and dark place. I truly believe if I'd had the means that night, I may have ended my life. I'd seen my business collapse, my friends had abandoned me, and my ambition evaporated into nothing. I was struggling, and my struggles meant my family was struggling. Worst of all, I just didn't see a way out.

That night, I looked around and saw just how far away success seemed and how impossible it felt to capture again. I was five years out from a period of astonishing success as a real estate broker. In those five years, I'd seen each of my four offices close, one after another. I'd seen my savings dry up and my opportunities dry up right along with them. Looking back, I could see painfully clearly how this period of difficulty was of my own making. I'd taken my success for granted and wasted my security and prosperity. Now, I was paying for those mistakes in full.

Left with so little, I couldn't find the drive to pick myself back up again. I was down, and down for the count. I was finished.

Or, so I thought.

In truth, I was only beginning. I was living through the struggle that would create the possibility for all my real and lasting success later. I was building up the foundation of strength I would need to fulfill my destiny and make my fortune. Amazingly, I already knew all that. I just didn't realize I knew it yet.

It was in that dark place that I recalled another dark night several years before. On that particular night, I'd awoken very early. I'd gotten up and found my way to a particular book, one I'd paged through until I'd found a particular story I'd felt I'd needed to read. It was the story of a particular man, a famous man, a man who might be the definition of success: David of Bethlehem.

That night, I opened my Bible and read 1 Samuel 16. It was there that I caught my first glimpse—then so obscure—of how to create a successful, full, and fulfilling life. The David I read about that night wasn't the great hero we all imagine when we hear the name. He wasn't mythological or historical or born out of an ancient or remote time. He wasn't the great king, the hero of war, or the writer of the Psalms. At least not yet. He was a hardworking boy doing a thankless job, trying to get by for his family. He was as real and present as you or me.

Yet, according to the text, David had all these abilities and skills lurking within him. He was a talented shepherd, a brilliant musician, an inspired military tactician, and an anointed king destined to rule over his people. Despite a future filled with so much glory, though, he wasn't aware that there was anything special about him. He didn't know there was anything more to him than meets the eye.

That little shepherd boy in 1 Samuel 16 had all the skills necessary to write his name in history. For all that talent, though, David's success was destined to be as much about how he used his struggles to grow wise and strong, allowing him to make the most of his skills when they were required. It's only because he pursued his success in a particular way that he was guaranteed all the success God had assigned for him.

Any scholar of the Bible can tell you that story. Anyone paying attention in church knows David started out a modest shepherd before rising higher. The revelation that came to me was more significant than that. What I realized was that David wasn't the only one blessed for so much success. There was a way to replicate that success in my life and in your life. Just understanding the path God has laid out for us would be enough for all of us to discover our many and various means of financial, personal, and spiritual fulfillment.

Reading on in the Good Book, and reading with far greater care than ever before, I discovered that David's path told us even more. It told us that we all have within us 12 Streams of Income and Fulfillment. The number and the path were very specific, but the opportunities they opened up could be infinite.

I didn't really understand all of this in that moment. I wasn't wise enough yet. I hadn't lived enough. The time wasn't right. So, I nestled the revelation in the back of my mind and continued on my foolish path.

A Rough Start

David didn't jump up and become king in an instant, either. For him to get that far, a lot of life had to happen. He had to meet with numerous setbacks and difficulties. He had to make mistakes and go through his trials and troubles to uncover what had already been discovered within him. He had to harden and strengthen himself up to be the fearsome and powerful leader he would become.

I, too, had to live through many trials and troubles before I could fully access the wisdom God was showing me. Even before my darkest night, I had already known a lot of struggle. I was raised by my grandparents, who both had trouble reading. Life wasn't easy for them or for me. My world was small, dangerous, and tough. There wasn't a lot of talk of success. The only role models I knew were people like my hustler father and the local drug dealers.

School wasn't an obvious path forward, either. The memory I have most from that period is scooting down as low as possible in my chair, trying to avoid catching my teacher's eye when she wanted someone to answer a question. I was just trying to get through my time at school, even though I didn't have that much to look forward to outside the classroom.

Simply put, I was brought up lost. I didn't have direction. Beyond my grandparents, I didn't have good role models. I was as wild as David must have been, spending all his time in the hills with his sheep.

Still, like David, there were certain core truths that marked me out for future opportunity. I'd been raised with drive by my grandparents. They taught me the value of working hard. The world had never been easy for them, and they didn't anticipate it getting any easier for me. Hard work was the only way to survive. My grandmother always told me you have to work twice as hard to come out even with the world. You've got to get up earlier than anyone else just to keep the field level. I still get up at 4 a.m. every day.

That drive opened up the path to becoming a real estate agent and my first period of success. For the first time in my life, I knew what it felt like to win at something. I discovered what it felt like to have not just enough to get by, but more than enough. I was able to afford the life I wanted to live and to help those I cared about. Yet, for some reason, while I was good at the work, I didn't feel fulfilled. Instead, I felt restless and dissatisfied. Success was great, but it wasn't enough. And so, I started making mistakes. I started playing around and losing focus.

And I was about to pay for it.

Seeing It All Go Wrong

At the time, I had two offices in the Philadelphia area and two in New Jersey, each doing bustling business. Things were going about as well as I thought they could, and I figured I could afford to take my eye off the ball for a bit. I figured I had earned the right to goof off. I leaned into that nameless sense of dissatisfaction, and I poured far too many of my resources into making fun the substitute for fulfillment. Instead of spending and saving my money responsibly, I was using my money to have a good time. Then, when the market took a bad turn, I wasn't prepared for it. The difficult times hit me, and they hit me hard.

One after another, I closed those four successful real estate offices. Very quickly, I went from a thriving businessman to a desperate one. I don't know if you've ever had to walk away from something you cared deeply about, but it's painful. We don't always get to choose how things end. We lose people, dreams, and jobs in life, whether we want to or not. This particular loss was definitely not voluntary. There was no way to delay and put this change on my schedule so I could do it in my time. It was thrust upon me, and because of that, I walked away from success and into the lowest moment of my life.

When I shut down my last office, I gave up on business and success. I didn't want to find another calling. I didn't want to look for a way back into real estate. I didn't want to do anything. Ever again. I had lost the great gift I'd inherited from my grandparents. I'd lost my drive for success.

That was all tough enough, but the losses kept coming. As soon as resources started getting tight, I discovered just who cared about me and who cared about my success. One friend said to my face, "I can no longer be your friend because you are beginning to fail." He wasn't the only one who felt that way, either. He was just the bluntest about it.

A Miracle Happened

That downward trend continued for five long years. Five years came and went, and I was no closer to finding my way back to the top. By then, my old success seemed a distant memory. That's when I started to think there was nothing left to look forward to in my life. I'd seen success, and I'd watched it get ripped out of my hands. I was no David after all. I was nobody.

At that point, if my family hadn't been there to inspire me to carry on, I may have found a way to give in and given up my life. As it was, when the test finally came, I found I still had enough strength left to carry on, if not for myself than for my wife and children.

And then, a miracle happened. Once I was past that dark moment, the revelation I had experienced long before began to return to my mind.

1 Samuel 16 beckoned me back, and I saw fully, for the first time, just what God wanted me to do.

I began searching for the Streams of Income and Fulfillment that I knew must exist within me. From a season of struggle, I hit upon a new season of searching, and eventually, a new path forward: network marketing. I got into the business, and I began seeing success for the first time in years. In no time, I was being feted with prizes, trips, and bonuses. I was rising up the ranks and becoming a major seller. Just as importantly, I was getting my confidence back.

There was only one hitch: try as I might, I couldn't get my network marketing income to match what I had been making in real estate. Before my revelation, that would have led to the return of that old feeling of discontent. I would have found myself looking for a way out instead of a way to make it work. Now that my revelation was firmly steering me, I knew precisely what I had to do.

I took my renewed confidence and returned to the ground where I had previously failed: real estate. I knew this wasn't the work I loved, but it was the work I could do best. I didn't abandon network marketing. I kept it, and I kept it in its place, where it could give me joy and income without inhibiting my ability to make what my family needed me to make.

Once I had opened these streams, things really started to flow in the right way. Doors just started opening. If I wanted to move on a particular venture, it became a success. If I wanted a particular space for a new office, that space became available, and at an affordable price.

Success became so automatic, it took me a moment realize the reason wasn't that I was a genius—it was that I was finally following the right path the right way.

Sharing the Streams

There's still a lot of my story left to write. There are streams I have yet to completely open for me—the most important of which is the writing of this book.

So many people need this revelation as much as I ever did. I meet people all the time, who are in that dark place I once found myself in. They're lost. They don't see a way to give their life meaning. They tell me, "Jack, you talk about 12 Streams of Income and Fulfillment, but I don't even have one."

I tell all of them the same thing: those twelve streams are there, and they are within you all the time. The key to your success is so accessible, and you can begin moving toward it this very minute.

I'm tired of seeing that same discontent I felt in my friends and neighbors. I don't want to keep these secrets to myself any longer. My grandparents taught me that success only matters when you share it with the people around you. I have a message that can change your life, and I need to make sure you hear it.

That message is a simple one. Wherever you are in your journey, your story is my story. And my story is David's story. I was born into difficulty, raised myself up, and then fell back down. It all had to happen so I could develop the strength necessary to follow through with the revelation I received.

I've experienced the good, the bad, and the ugly, just as you have. I had to experience it all to find the foundations on which to build my success. I work in real estate, and I can tell you, nothing you put up stays up if it isn't built on a firm, strong foundation. In my earlier years, my foundation was shaky, uneven, and liable to crumble. It took a lot of tough lessons to put me on the solid ground I'm on today, in a place where I can confidently share the secrets to a truly fulfilling life.

We have to stop looking at struggle as a sign that we aren't living right and see it for what it is: the way we build the strength and wisdom necessary to discover our full potential. Whether you're in the midst of a struggle, fearing one ahead, or just on the other side of one, David's story shows that you aren't a fool and your future doesn't have to be disappointing. There's a king or queen inside you. You just need to know how to get him or her out.

There Is a Way Forward

This book was inspired by God, but it isn't just for the godly. It's for anyone who is still living with discontent and looking for their sense of fulfillment. It's for those people who have been through their troubles or see them ahead, and who need to know there's a way forward. Most importantly, it's for those who feel they have something to give the world but who just don't know how to give it yet.

Despite what it can feel like in the moment, I'm here to tell you: your situation and circumstances are not here to destroy you. They are here to make you strong enough to succeed and discover your full potential. When difficulty comes to pass, it hasn't come forever, but it has come with a purpose. The trick is in knowing how to use what you learn from that difficulty to fuel the release of your 12 Streams of Income and Fulfillment.

I know you've experienced trials in your own life. I know there have been moments it felt like you couldn't ever achieve what you dreamed of. You may be in one of those moments right now. But you don't have to despair as I once did. You have the strength within you to bring together your talents, gifts, pleasures, and purpose to make your life whole and purposeful.

That strength comes from the heavy weight you've been carrying. If you know how to use it, those difficulties are the foundations upon which you will build your success. All you need to know is how to make sturdy walls out of all that weight you've been carrying, and I'm here to tell you how.

This book is going to show you how to transform the trials in your life into triumphs. I'll guide you to a place where you are not only working to get by, but also discovering new levels of financial and personal success, all the while making a meaningful contribution to the world and experiencing true fulfillment. We'll make our way step-by-step from the corner you feel you're stuck in to a wide-open world full of infinite possibility.

Are you ready for that? Then, let's get to it.

Consider your life as a whole. Where can you see God working through your life? Think of how you can redefine your difficult moments as strengths that build toward God's plan for you.

_____

_____

_____

_____

_____

_____

_____

_____

_____

SECTION I.

THE 12 WALLS THAT

SUPPORT YOU

CHAPTER 1

The 12 Walls that Struggle Built

Before we can jump into the revelation that is going to change your life, I want to start by talking a little about visualization. If you don't know what visualization is, it's a way to use your mind to reimagine the world in a particular way. It is built upon two powerful mental tools: the law of manifestation and the law of attraction.

The law of manifestation states that nothing exists until we make it. Our goals, our dreams, our perfect job…: none of that exists until we think it does. When we become focused on an idea, we create it—or manifest it—in the world. The law of attraction is similar in some ways. It states that what we think about most is drawn to us. All the time, we're pulling opportunities or difficulties toward us depending on how we're thinking. Imagine this law as a magnet. Place one pole of a magnet on a table, and it attracts certain metals. Place the other end on the table, and it repels them. Similarly, if we think of those positive changes we want, we draw them toward us. When we concentrate on negative thinking, we draw those negatives toward us instead.

At first, these two laws may seem to conflict. How can I be manifesting things in the world and also attracting them?

I'm going to tell you how.

Your thoughts are powerful. If you focus your mind on finding a job in marketing, your mind puts that potential out in the world. Focusing your thoughts on that marketing job *creates* the opportunities while simultaneously *drawing* them toward you.

Conversely, if you spend all your time thinking about your difficulties, your mind creates new problems and draws them toward you. Soon, it isn't just that you have a job you don't like—your negative thinking may have created a problem with your spouse or romantic partner. You've created that problem and put it in the world. And then, by continuing to think like that, you attract that problem until it's clinging to your life.

Basically, we have to be careful how we think. We need to learn not only to follow the standard steps to finding our abundance in life, but also to learn to think, imagine, and focus in a new way.

That's where visualization comes in. By constructing visual ideas in our minds, we focus our thoughts more easily on these positive changes we want. As we all know, when we daydream, our brains switch into visual mode. We see people, places, and objects. By visualizing, we key into that process. Visualizing your perfect home makes it easier for your mind to manifest and attract that home into your life. It's much easier than just telling yourself, "I'd really like a home."

To home in on both of these powers, we're going to use a lot of visualization in this book. I'll walk you through an extended visualization exercise that takes you from where you are at this very moment right to your 12 Streams of Income and Fulfillment.

So, let's get started.

The House on the Hill

I want you to imagine a hilltop out in wide open country. Around you, at a little distance down the hill, are blue, flowing streams full of fresh, life-giving water. In the water, shimmery nuggets of precious metals, ripe for you to reach in and grasp. Your goal is to get to and utilize each and every one of those streams. Those are your Streams of Income and Fulfillment.

Right now, though, you're alone on this hilltop and instead of being outside in the fresh air and sunshine, you're inside a huge house. While the rooms are fairly comfortable, you aren't enjoying the comfort and security of the home. Instead, you're sitting in the darkest corner in the room farthest from the front of the house, where all your windows are. Instead of getting up, stretching your legs, and getting some fresh air, you feel trapped in that corner. You don't know how to get out of it. The only window you can see from that corner is dust-covered and locked. From the perspective of your corner, looking at that window, the outside appears murky and uninviting. You can't see the streams below or even the blue sky above. While you've heard from others that there's a way out and the world outside is pleasant and refreshing, from where you're sitting, it doesn't really feel that way.

Are you with me so far? I don't want you to get weighed down by that corner right now. That's where we all start, but this book is going to get you out of it. We're going to get you to those streams, but we've got to start by recognizing just where we are right now. We're in a corner, and it's one of our own making. No one has put us here. No one has forced us into this corner. We've been building this house on top of this hill our whole lives. In fact, each one of these walls has been built up over time by our own choices, creating the vast enclosure we now feel trapped in. Every misstep in our lives, every mistake, and every bad choice has gone into the foundation that supports these walls. At one point, these walls felt light and airy, like those paper walls in a Japanese home. By now, though, they're so thick and strong, they feel like a prison.

Here's the thing though; these walls may feel like they're trapping you right now, but what they're really doing is giving you a base of strength. The difference between a prison and a home is that you can leave a home. And you can leave this place whenever you want. The only one keeping you in here is you.

Once you realize that, you can begin to see that these walls aren't all bad. They've kept the wind out. They've kept you dry. More than that, they've allowed you to grow strong while building them up. These walls around you are actually your strength, the base from which you can launch yourself on your adventure and discover those streams.

Meeting Your Walls

In this first section, we're going to go over each one of these walls individually to reacquaint you with the home you've built for yourself. We'll find out where the initial issue that became this wall came from, and we're going to discover why that strong boundary can actually be beneficial as you prepare to get out into the world and find those 12 Streams of Income and Fulfillment.

Not everyone reading this book will have all twelve of these walls in their home. Some of you will have more than twelve. Some of you will have half of that. Wherever you are in the building process, I want you to know that you're in the right place right now.

If you haven't been through some of these, keep living. If you've been through more than enough, keep living as well. This foundation is going to be laid. These walls are going to go up. There's no avoiding the struggle that comes with building these rooms for yourself.

You may not have enjoyed going through any of these twelve events in your life. If you have some ahead, you still won't enjoy them, even if you know what's coming. That's okay. These walls are making you stronger and preparing you for what you really need to be doing in life. Without these walls, you can't get to those streams outside.

That's just a part of life. Accept it. Don't fight it. Allow it and learn by it. Know that this is part of building a better you.

CHAPTER 2

Room 1: The Walls the World Puts Up

We've got a lot of walls around us. If you were just trapped in a single room, you probably would have found your way out the door by now. Instead, this place you're in feels twisted. You might find the courage and strength to get up and peak around a corner, but if all you find waiting for you are more walls, more halls, more dark passages that don't seem to lead anywhere, you'd probably get discouraged and sit back down in your corner.

To really gain a picture of the walls around us, and how to navigate our way through them, we need to break them up into sections—or rooms—so they feel more tamable. So, let's start with that first room and make our way from there.

In this chapter, we'll cover the first four walls. These are the walls that the world has put up around you. If you've done any living at all, you've probably encountered these walls. These walls come gratis with almost every life. Because they're so fundamental to every life, they're really the innermost room in the house, the heart of the obstacles that have kept us from discovering our 12 Streams of Income and Fulfillment.

Our first goal, then, is to get to know these walls and to discover the strength they have provided us. Then, we'll be able to get up and make more progress in getting out.

Wall 1: Facing Your Adversity

It would be nice if life were easy, wouldn't it? Ideally, every time we set a goal, things would just align around us and push us to success. If that were the case, we'd all already be rich and feel completely fulfilled in our chosen work.

Unfortunately, life doesn't tend to make things that easy for us. Instead, as soon as we try to do anything of significance in our lives (and sometimes when we're just trying to get by), all of a sudden, we're caught in quicksand. Not only are we not making progress, we're sinking down. Progress feels impossible, and soon, just staying afloat seems like more than we can handle.

I know what I'm talking about with adversity. I was dropped into my grandmother's arms when I was two weeks old because my mother wasn't able to care for me. Her mother told her that she couldn't bring another child into the house. On a Friday evening, when my grandmother was preparing to go out and have a nice time at a cabaret, my mother knocked on the door, and said, "I can't keep him. I want you to raise him."

My grandmother didn't hesitate. She took me in immediately. When my grandfather came home and asked how they were going to take care of me, she told him, "I don't know, but we're going to do it."

My grandmother saved me—the first but not the last woman to do so—and gave me a chance at life. But the consequences of that moment still left me facing a lot of obstacles. I still faced a childhood in the inner city, one full of violence, drugs, and limited chances. So, adversity isn't just a word to me; it's a whole section of my biography.

I'm not bragging. We've all been tested and struggled in life. Those times were tough for me, and your struggles were tough for you. It isn't a competition. Our adversity, whatever it is, is always incredibly difficult. Those struggles calcify and make this first wall in our room. It's about as tough and solid and strong as structures come.

Looking along this wall, you'll see all the scars of constantly running into it. There are scratch marks and cracks where you pounded on this wall. It never budged.

But you know what? This tough and solid and strong structure has made us tough and solid and strong as well. I want you to look at this wall—at your history of adversity—and stop seeing it as an impediment to your success. Instead, I want you to see it for what it is: the key ingredient to what made you as strong as you are today. Tough times made you stronger, and that strength is what is going to get you up now, so you can get going and succeed.

Most of us chronically underestimate ourselves and how strong we are. We see this first wall in front of us, and we see failure in the face of tough odds. Instead, we should see increasing strength and resilience. You've been strong enough to keep going against all your adversities. You've pulled yourself out of quicksand over and over again. Though you've yet to get across the pit to where your dreams reside, every time you've tested yourself in that quicksand, you've become a stronger swimmer.

In fact, just reading this book is a sign of your strength. You're strong enough to try again and to try a new way forward.

This strength is leading somewhere. There's something inside you. There's a purpose that is seeking expression.

You have this power and purpose, but you may not know what it is yet. That's okay. We're working toward it. What's important to know here is that you have this strength within you, even if you don't see it yet.

Wall 2: Losing Your Support

Wasn't there supposed to be a bench on this wall? There was supposed to be a bed or a couch over here. There was supposed to be something to lean on, to rest on, and to rely on when things got tough. Yet, when you needed that help, after facing your adversity, you found it empty.

Maybe that's not the case for you; maybe there's a comfortable seat right there on the wall waiting for you, but you just don't want to take the seat. You feel like that's a sign you aren't strong enough, like it proves you're too weak to stand on your own two feet. So, you just stand there, exhausted, stumbling, half-fainting, while you refuse to take advantage of what is right in front of you.

I've got news for you, tough guy: times come along in every life when you have to lean on something or somebody. No one is tough enough to conquer life alone. We're going to get beaten up by adversity. We're going to make mistakes (plenty of them in the next couple rooms). We're going to get tired and discouraged. In those times, you have to lean on something to catch your breath.

What does that support look like? It's different for each person. For some, it's a close friend. Others rely on parents or mentors. You may rely on your spouse in tough times, or you may rely on your children to inspire strength in you. When all else fails, there is someone you can always lean on: God Himself.

Whatever your source of support, you've got to become comfortable relying on it in the moments you need it. That requires a lot of honesty with yourself and with others. You have to learn how to ask for help and how to take it.

When I was a young man, I found myself in a difficult position. I had two daughters, and I was involved in some very bad business. I'd been selling drugs for a while as a quick way to prosperity, and that choice was taking its toll. After taking that wrong turn early in life, I was nearing a dead end at that point. I needed to restart my life and get on the right track.

But I couldn't do that on my own. It was too much for one man to do, whoever that man may be. To do it, I needed God, and I needed my daughters. I often tell my second daughter that she saved my life because it was after her birth that I found the strength to quit the world of drugs, which had been so prominent in my life until then. It was because of that choice that I found my way into real estate.

Again, I couldn't have done it alone. I needed her to inspire and strengthen me, and I needed God to guide me. I needed God to tell me, "This is the way; walk in it."

Sometimes, you've got to lean on this wall of support when things are going rough. If you've tried to handle it all on your own without support, you've already learned this lesson well. At the same time, sometimes, you also need this wall when things are going a little too well. It's easy to get a big head when you finally have a pocket full of money. The support in your life is there not just to keep you from falling when things are bad; it's to keep your feet on the ground when things are good.

What do you do, though, when that support seems to abandon you? There are times we all go through when this wall feels like it's a false wall, ready to crumble if you put any weight on it. Suddenly, after a particularly tough moment of adversity, you begin to question if you have any true friends and if your family really cares. You begin to think people only cared about you because you looked strong and successful.

As I related earlier, in one of the toughest moments of my life, I once had a friend tell me to my face, "I can't be friends with you anymore because you are beginning to fail."

When I needed that friend the most, he turned his back on me. I went to lean in, and he let me fall.

What I learned from that, though, was that we really have to recognize what kind of friends we have in our lives. Some of our friends are there for a reason, some for a season, and some are there for life. Learning the difference allows us to know who we can lean on in those tough moments.

At the same time as that friend abandoned me, my pastor was there to help me. My family was there to help me. Other friends stood by me even as things got temporarily worse.

I'm here to tell you that the picture you paint of your life, as a person with no one reliable who you can lean on, is almost certainly false. Most people have more support than they realize. One friend may abandon you. Another may, too, but there are people out there who will love and support you through anything. If you don't know them yet, it's time to go meet them. Make a priority of finding a community of support, whether it's a church, a club, or a neighbor.

The truth is anyone who has felt this wall give way in a tough moment knows that you need this wall, no matter how strong you are. David wouldn't have gotten very far if he hadn't had Samuel and Jonathan there to help him early in his life, and no one ever accused David of being weak.

You have that support somewhere in your life, whether it's family, friends, your church, or just God. Get comfortable relying upon that support as a part of your journey out of this room and into your success.

Wall 3: Losing Your Home

In some particularly tough moments, you aren't just struggling to find a friend to lean on; you're struggling to find a home to shelter yourself in.

Now, I'm not just talking literally about the house you live in, although plenty of us have spent time without a set of walls we can call our own as well. When I say home, I mean something much broader. I'm talking about that zone of comfort you've built up to feel safe and secure. Your home is the collection of things that provide you protection and meaning in life. That can be your house, but it can also be your business or the people around you who give you a sense of peace and support. It can even be the persona you've constructed that you use to shelter yourself from painful confrontations. Your home, then, has more to do with your identity and how you support that identity than just the building you keep your stuff in.

When you lose your home, you lose a real sense of who you are. You lose that sense of where you belong and why you do what you do. When I lost my real estate business after the financial crash, I felt homeless. Emotionally, spiritually, I was a drifter. I had nowhere to go. I had no mission anymore, no sense of protection. I went from feeling invulnerable within the walls of my business life to feeling like I was completely vulnerable to every threat around every corner.

It was only when another part of my sphere of comfort stepped up, when my family came to my rescue and sheltered me that I was slowly able to recover and rebuild.

At the time, losing your home is, of course, incredibly difficult. You will inevitably feel, at very least, uncomfortable with your circumstances, and you may feel—as I did—outright lost (more on that with Wall 4). It can take years to rebuild after you lose your home, and if you are also struggling with Wall 2 at the same time, it can be a particularly trying experience (crushing even, as we're about to see).

But there's a lot of wisdom that comes from running into this wall as well. After all, the reason we often lose our homes is because we didn't appreciate what we had at the time. In my case, I wasn't paying enough attention to the basics of my business. I didn't appreciate the risks I was taking, and I was trying to achieve it all too quickly and without enough focus. Afterward, though, you can bet I learned that lesson.

In other words, I wasn't handling my basic home maintenance. I wasn't keeping the bushes trimmed and the grass cut. I wasn't keeping up with the plumbing and electric. I wasn't even paying my mortgage in full. I was enjoying the benefit of my home without doing what it took to keep my home. And so, I lost it for a while. Now, I know never to forget those responsibilities again.

That's the positive side of losing your home. Whether it's an apartment or house, a business, an opportunity, a person, or a sense of yourself, losing your home shows you in the most brutal way imaginable that you were not doing enough to safeguard your peace.

Like a forest fire that leaves the regrown forest stronger and more resilient, losing your home allows you to rebuild a stronger and more grounded you, one who appreciates more fully what you have in your life. The foundations for this wall will be far more solid now, and you'll be able to remain more focused and centered because of what you went through.

Wall 4: Getting Crushed

Sometimes, life doesn't just take it all out of you through adversity; it takes it all out and then takes a little more. Sometimes, someone comes and takes your home. Sometimes, a rock falls on it and crushes it. Or, more likely, that rock has fallen on you.

When you lose your home, you lose a comfort, something that made you feel secure in yourself and your place in the world. When you get crushed, you just lose everything.

These can be one and the same event. For me, losing all I'd built in my real estate business, it didn't just take away that sense of comfort that came with my good income and my good job; it took away my sense of being. It took away who I thought I was. In other words, it crushed me. I don't know how many days I just sat around, not looking for a way back into the business, not looking for the way into any business. I wasn't looking to get back to success; I was done with it. I didn't want to do anything.

When you're crushed, it has a lot to do with the circumstances of the event. You can end up homeless or without a person to lean on, but in a way that is on your terms. You got the eviction notice, but you get to decide when you go. When you're crushed, you don't make a choice to step away from where you were comfortable, you are forced out by some catastrophe.

This wasn't deciding to step away from a job because it felt like too much. It wasn't walking away from a relationship because it wasn't nurturing your needs. This is getting fired. This is getting dumped. And what's more, it's coming back to your desk or your home and finding your stuff packed up for you and a note saying, "Get Out." When you're crushed, it's sudden, and it's overwhelming.

To say this is one of the hardest moments of your life is a little redundant. No one gets crushed and just gets right back up, dusts themselves off, and gets back to what they were doing before. This isn't a cartoon where a boulder can fall on you and you just bounce right back up. No, when you're crushed, you're broken. And you're going to need a lot of time to heal.

In the moment, when you've just been hit by that Mack truck and you're lying on the pavement, shattered, you probably feel like there's no good to come from this wall. I know I felt that way. Getting crushed feels like it's just pain and setbacks. But that isn't the case.

Even this wall has a lot to give you, a lot of strength to offer you, so you can reinforce yourself and succeed now. Because if you were crushed in the past, the fact is, you did get better. The human spirit is incredibly resilient. It gets hit, and it can get back up, no matter what was thrown at it. It may have taken a while to heal, but you did heal. You got back up. That's why you're reading this book.

Getting crushed and getting back up teaches us that it is always possible to rebuild, that we can find a way back no matter how hard we've been knocked down.

You can think of this wall as one that fell on you and broke you, but it's also a wall that proved you could get up and fix yourself. You've proven to yourself in the past that you have the incredible strength to pick yourself back up after the worst happened. How can you doubt now you have the strength to get out of that corner you're in and get to your 12 Streams of Income and Fulfillment?

Write out a description of your first four walls. Detail what happened, how those events have affected you, and whether you have overcome them and moved on.

Wall 1:

_____

_____

_____

_____

Wall 2:

_____

_____

_____

_____

Wall 3:

_____

_____

_____

_____

Wall 4:

_____

_____

_____

_____

Now, write about them not as obstacles that have kept you in a corner but as moments that have allowed you build strength, support, appreciativeness, and wisdom today.

_____

_____

_____

_____

_____

_____

_____

_____

CHAPTER 3

Room 2:
The Walls You Made Yourself

With the first four walls, you were faced with circumstances that were in many ways beyond your control. That's not to say you didn't play your part in losing your home or getting crushed. You may have been thoughtless or irresponsible, as I was in my past. But, ultimately, you didn't choose for those struggles to come to you. You didn't make the choice for those challenges to meet you.

In that sense, the first four walls were something like natural disasters. Sure, you could have built those walls to better resist the hurricane winds that came blowing, but you didn't choose for your home to be in the path of the hurricane.

What separates those walls from the next four, then, is how much responsibility you have for them. In the first four, troubled times came for you. Here, these walls are largely your missteps along the path in life.

I don't want to imply you've done wrong by building these walls. They were the natural result of the difficulties and opportunities you faced. But we also need to transform those choices from the mistakes of the past into the strengths of today.

We've made it out of that corner in that first room at this point. We're entering a new room that's a little airier, a little cleaner, a little larger. We can see a little light from the front of the house shining through. We're stronger and more focused, but we still have a way to go.

Wall 5: Misspending Your Abundance

Not every setback comes when you're down. Sometimes, it's not how you've reacted to misfortune; it's how you've reacted to fortune.

You just got that big raise you worked hard for over the last few years, and what did you do with it? Did you put some money away in savings, pay down your debts, invest in a long-cherished dream, or share it with those who really needed it? No, you bought the fancy car, bought an expensive new wardrobe, picked up some unhealthy, expensive habits, or went on a vacation that was way beyond what you could afford.

It can happen to any of us. When we work so hard to reach abundance, we can overcorrect after years of tightening our belts and making sacrifices. That first taste of success, and we're off thinking we've won the lottery. We lose our heads, and then, a little later, we pay for it.

Take a look at this wall. You can see the signs of former expensive treats you purchased yourself there. There are the lines where expensive paintings used to hang and pictures of expensive purchases and travels. You can make out where you used to hang all those expensive clothes you had to pawn off. Looking over this wall, you might at first just feel regret, but you'd be missing the powerful lesson those marks are showing you.

I know what I'm talking about. I've lived in a single room in the center of the inner city. I've also splurged on a 5,000-square-foot house. Could I afford that home? Could I be sure to keep it if the abundance disappeared on me? You know the answer already. I thought getting to abundance was like crossing the finish line: once you get there, you've made it and there's no going back. I didn't realize that success was something that can disappear as suddenly as it appeared.

We live for those moments of abundance, the moments in life when everything is great. Your finances are great, your love life is great, your family isn't fighting, your future is looking bright, etc. Everything is going great.

But we have to remember that "this too shall pass." We have to learn to be grateful and enjoy abundance when it arrives and to avoid fooling ourselves into thinking a period of favor guarantees a lifetime without struggle.

It's okay if you were a fool when you had abundance. That's part of the process. We just don't want to remain a fool. We want to be wise the next time we taste abundance. Because we're heading in the direction of abundance again. And this time, we want it to last.

Tasting the fruits of abundance and the bitter wine of failure go hand-in-hand to teach us some very valuable lessons. They teach us to be more careful with our financial, mental, and spiritual resources. They teach us to be grateful and to plan ahead as nothing lasts forever.

I'm grateful I have lived in a huge home. I'm also grateful I had to move back to a single room. Both of those experiences have made me stronger and wiser.

Wall 6: Spreading Yourself Too Thin

How do you get to that taste of abundance? It's a question I know you've asked. That's part of why you're here. If you already knew the way to your 12 Streams of Income and Fulfillment, you'd have discovered them on your own. That's the beauty of this system. You can find your way on your own… once you've got the map.

Abundance involves a lot of work, some luck, and a lot of wisdom. Whether you're in a period of abundance, searching your way back to former abundance, or chasing your first taste, I can tell something else about you: you're probably spreading yourself too thin. You've got too many jobs, too many commitments. You've made too many promises you feel you can't walk back on. You've got too many obligations, too many debts, and a schedule that's far too full.

I know you're struggling with this because this wall is a part of modern life. We live on a 24/7/365 schedule now. To begin with, we're working more than in previous generations. There was a time when people got to work at nine, finished at five, and then enjoyed their evenings and weekends. That's not this time. Even those of us lucky enough to have a single job and a good schedule have to deal with businesses that demand far more from us for every hour of work and every dollar they pay us. It exhausts us, and it strips us of the resources we need to move forward with our lives.

You have to ask yourself: how can you get the right jobs and make the right income if you don't have the resources to get beyond today?

Work is a lot harder than it used to be, and at the same time, we're also dealing with the timeless demands of families, friends, churches, and communities. We're pulled in every direction, every step of the way.

Looking over this wall, you can see a clutter of schedules and notes reminding you of all you have to do. There's a calendar that is almost illegible with all the reminders on it. There are lists everywhere for everything you have to remember to do today, tomorrow, next week, next month, and onward. Just looking at it can be exhausting, but getting beyond the details, you can see a valuable lesson amongst all those scribbles.

That lesson is simple. Take a big red marker and write across the whole wall the word "no."

We don't always have control over our work situation. Sometimes, we have to put those extra hours in because we have to be able to pay those bills and take care of our families. However, there are plenty of opportunities, even at work, where we could really benefit from a lesson I learned from my grandmother: "No is okay sometimes."

We all want to say "yes" to everybody. We want to be all things to all people, and we want to be able to make everyone happy and give everything to everybody.

If you've been overcommitted, stressed, gotten burned out from trying to say "yes" to everyone who asks something of you, then you're in a position to learn one of the most valuable lessons in this book. You are a valuable commodity, and you have to take care of how much you share of yourself. So, just say "no" when a commitment is too much.

Saying "no" when what is asked of you is beyond your time, energy, or abilities isn't offensive. It isn't letting people down. The only way you can let anyone down is by overpromising and then getting burned out before you can deliver. If someone asks you to drive them to work at five in the morning when you work until ten at night, you can say "yes" and run yourself down until you're sick. Or, you can say "no," and they can find someone else to do it. Don't let others pressure you into overwhelming yourself.

This lesson is crucial because when we get to the 12 Streams, you may try to overcommit yourself. You need to know your limitations before you get to that success, so you can apportion yourself out depending on your strength at the time.

Wall 7: Backsliding

Misusing our abundance, overstretching ourselves: these issues can lead to a very common mistake: the backslide.

We've all had backslide moments in our lives. We go back to that former partner, even though we know they're no good for us. We go back to the old job we quit, even though we hated the work and the boss. We move back home because making our own way somewhere else has just gotten too tough. It all ends the same way it did the first time: badly.

Once we get away again, we know it was wrong. We can see quite clearly we were just looking for something familiar to give us a little comfort. Sure, that relationship was bad, but we're lonely. We're afraid we'll never find someone better. Yes, the job was bad, but we've lost our confidence in ourselves that we could ever do better. Of course, we don't want to move home, but we've convinced ourselves we can't do it on our own anymore.

You can see from all those examples what is at the heart of backsliding. It's a lack of self-confidence in the face of setbacks. This wall reflects those feelings. It's full of old, dusty mistakes that we keep picking up, cleaning off again, and trying to make something into something else. This wall is really all the things we want to get away from. For some reason, though, we just can't convince ourselves to throw all the junk away and put up goals for the future instead.

I've heard people call themselves failures because of this, but you don't need to be so hard on yourself. Like I said, we've all done this. I moved back to the inner city with my two daughters after my divorce. Years later, I slipped backwards and had to work for my daughter instead of running my own company. It's okay. This is also a part of building up the strong foundations we need to move forward.

These failures, these weaknesses of judgment, will end up making us stronger and more self-aware. How? It's only when we fall back that we can realize where we've been and where we need to head. You can never know in life where you are until you have something that's set you back. Only then do you know how good it was and how good it could be.

Think about it like this. You don't miss the relationship, the job, or the old home; you miss what you had in those moments. You miss the comfort of love and support in a relationship, the financial security in the job, the lack of stress about your basic needs in the home. Instead of seeking these out by going back to what didn't work, you can see what you need to find elsewhere going forward. More than that, you can see that you've achieved those things before in your life, so you can achieve them again.

You don't want that old relationship; you want a new one, one that is built on a better foundation and more likely to prosper. You don't want the old, dysfunctional job; you want a better place of employment that will also pay you what you're worth and treat you how you deserve. You don't want the old home; you want to build a new home for yourself.

This wall, then, is teaching you what you're looking for in life, and it's also showing you that you can get that for yourself. You don't have to look to the past; the future has far more to offer you.

Wall 8: Being Broken

In the last chapter, we concluded with getting crushed by your circumstances. Here, we're in the same territory, only now we're broken.

When you make a lot of poor decisions—like misspending your abundance, stretching yourself too thin, and backsliding in an unhelpful direction—you are still in the realm of quick recovery. You've still got something left in you to fight your way back after those bad choices. Being broken, on the other hand, leaves you with nothing.

This isn't backsliding. This isn't you making a bad choice and taking the wrong path backward. Backsliding allows you to see the way back forward. Broken is when you can't see anything.

You can't see tomorrow. You can't imagine tomorrow. In fact, when you're broken, you don't even want tomorrow to come.

In the introduction, I detailed the moment I was broken. In my darkest nights, the time I was contemplating ending it all; that's the kind of broken I'm talking about. It isn't always suicidal, but it is always that desperate. There are moments when we feel there's just no way forward. Our spirits are shattered, and we can't get back up again.

If we imagine this wall, what we see is…nothing. There's nothing here to draw from. It's a moment of complete emptiness and helplessness. Sometimes, it's brought on by the loss of a whole career, all of our earning potential. Sometimes, it's due to a turn in our health, like the loss of our physical capabilities. Other times, it involves the loss of a loved one in some permanent sense, either a partner walking away forever or because of the true forever, death.

In such moments, our minds respond in the only way they can: they break.

The thing is, sometimes a break is necessary to make the healing better. Doctors will re-break bones sometimes if they don't set right. The immediate pain is necessary so that the healing will be thorough.

If you've ever broken a bone, you know it's more than painful; it's frustrating. You can't do the things you're used to doing. You can't do the things you like to do and would like to do. But how much more grateful are you once you're healed again? How much do you enjoy being able to walk on your own or go for a run? How wonderful to be able to use your hand to throw a ball or write a simple note!

That gratitude, that appreciation for what you can do, what you are capable of, even in ordinary life, shouldn't be underestimated. Being broken and working toward being healed invests you with a greater strength of character, and a greater wisdom.

When we work out, we are aiming to build stronger muscles. To do that, though, we have to push our muscle fibers until they are damaged. That damage is what allows muscles to grow. The damage leads to stronger muscles. We break ourselves to get stronger. It's the only way it works.

You have to be broken to come back stronger, like heating steel in the flame to make it solid enough to cut through anything. Without facing this intense difficulty, you just won't have the toughness to get from here to your 12 Streams of Income and Fulfillment.

Write out a description of your second set of walls. Detail what happened, how those events have affected you, and whether you have overcome them and moved on.

Wall 5:

_____

_____

_____

_____

Wall 6:

_____

_____

_____

_____

Wall 7:

_____

_____

_____

_____

Wall 8:

_____

_____

_____

_____

Now, write about them not as obstacles that have kept you in a corner but as moments that have allowed you to become wiser and stronger.

_____

_____

_____

_____

_____

_____

_____

_____

_____

CHAPTER 4

Room 3: The Walls You Built to Protect Yourself

The first room we found ourselves in had walls we had no control over. The outside world affected us, and sometimes it affected us negatively. We could only do so much about that. The second room involved our reactions to different opportunities and difficult circumstances. We misused our successes, spread ourselves thin trying to take every opportunity and please everyone, tried to go backward in life to recapture what we once had, and broke ourselves on our struggles. In other words, we made some mistakes in our judgment.

When we're recovering from those four walls, though, we often build up a final four, the last four in this building we've constructed. These walls, though, are neither from the world nor our immediate reaction to our circumstances. Instead, they're the walls we build up to ensure the setbacks of the first two rooms never come back for us again. These walls change our relationship with others and the world. If we live within a castle of our own making, these are the defensive wall, the drawbridge, and the moat. We've built these walls so we hide within and fight off anything that comes to harm us again.

In the context of trying to leave this house, that can sound like a negative, but as we've already seen with other walls, there are a lot of positive qualities we can take from these defensive choices.

In fact, once we understand and take advantage of these walls, we are that much closer to getting outside and finding our 12 Streams of Income and Fulfillment. By uncovering the foundations of these walls and how they have strengthened instead of setting us back, we'll finally have the toughness to move forward with our journey.

We're in the front room of this building we've created. We have the sun streaming in through the windows. The outdoors is so close. The streams are close. To get outside though, we'll first have to cross the room and get to the locked door (more on that in the next section). For now, let's get to know more about this room so we can take all the strength and lessons it has to offer.

Wall 9: Feeling Under Siege

When things go wrong, you can start to feel like the whole world is against you. Your friends aren't on your side. Your coworkers are conspiring against you. Your family is tired of hearing your complaints. Even luck is against you. Every part of your life has come together to make things tough and make achievement impossible.

In that moment, the most obvious reaction, the most reasonable way to behave, is to build up your walls and prepare for a full-on siege. If you look along this wall, you'll see images of a vast conspiracy. There will be a list of all that has gone wrong—all the ways you've been wronged—and explanations tying everything together. To others, this wall will look as crazy as those conspiracy maps connected with string in Hollywood movies, but to you, it's just a sign of the truth.

Feeling under siege leads to one obvious reaction to the world: it closes you off. You stop looking for a new job because you don't believe anyone will ever give you one. You stop talking to friends and family because you don't believe they'll support you. You don't share your despair or your suspicions, and so both get locked up inside you and continue to expand, taking over everything.

You may end up walking away from important relationships or opportunities just because you've lost trust in the world. Friends who intend to help you through these moments can find their calls unanswered and the door shut and locked in their face. You may become short, unpleasant, and always on the defensive, looking for ways to be offended and angry.

What's even worse, because we cut ourselves off from others, we make it that much harder to pull ourselves out of this difficult position. Where we might otherwise count on those whom we love to support us and lift us back up, once we cut them off, we leave ourselves alone, without anyone to help.

In the moment, that makes this experience even bleaker, but there is a sunnier side to this wall. This wall teaches us to be independent and to rely upon ourselves. It's easy sometimes to become addicted to getting assistance from others. We start relying on it even when we don't truly need it. That can end up holding us back because we become afraid to venture out and take on challenges on our own.

When we go through this moment, we cut too many ties, but we also force ourselves to rise up again on our own. We learn just how much strength we possess and how much we can achieve on our own. When seeking our personal, individual path to our 12 Streams of Income and Fulfillment, that lesson is invaluable.

At the same time, we also develop a healthy amount of skepticism. While we may be wrong to cut everyone off and suspect everyone when we go through this, we have to learn not to trust every word spoken to us. After all, as I've already discussed, not every friend is a true friend for life. Not everyone we work with has our best interests or the best interests of the company at heart. Learning to detect who is genuine and means to help and who isn't and doesn't is critical to our continued rise.

Wall 10: The Rock in You That Has Caused Division

When you face struggles, there is often one thing popping up over and over again that you will say to yourself, "I'll give up everything but this." Your "this" may be a business, a goal, an idea, a belief, an intention, or any number of other things. For our purposes, whatever your "this" is, it's your rock.

"Take everything," you tell the world, "but I'm going to cling to this rock."

Why do we do that? Why do we pick one rock and stick to it? For one thing, rocks are big, heavy, sturdy things. Jesus Christ built the church upon the man he named Peter, or "the rock." Why? Because that rock wasn't going to ever move, not for anybody. Just as we might pull up the drawbridge under siege, we would grasp for a sturdy rock when the waves come in heavy during a storm on the beach. If anything is going to outlast the storm, it'll be that rock. It's just simple, smart survival instinct to cling on to what we believe is stronger than us.

That may be a smart survival tactic, but once the storm has passed, you run into a very obvious problem. If you keep clinging to that rock, you'll never get off the beach again.

In less metaphorical terms, if you cling to one thing above all else, you lose that crucial flexibility you need to be able to make changes in your life and adapt to new circumstances.

When I had four real estate offices open and things started going wrong, I could have adapted, slimmed down the organization, and worked on a smaller scale until things turned around. Instead, I clung to my rock. "I'm never closing any of these offices."

I thought I was being smart. I thought I was doing the right thing when the storm approached. Instead, if I'd let go of that rock, I could have outrun the storm. As it was, clinging to that rock meant I saw it all get washed away. I didn't lose one office. I lost all four.

Plenty of others will have seen a marriage washed away in the same way, or a close friendship, or a dream they had long cherished. It's somewhat counterintuitive, but the more we cling to such things, the more we actually run the risk of losing them. We become too stubborn to adapt to the world around us, and it costs us dearly.

Looking at this wall, with an enormous rock leaning against it, you can be forgiven for seeing nothing but an obstacle now. You became stubborn, dug in, and clung to a rock, and it cost you.

But, as with all the other walls in this structure, you've actually become far stronger because of this experience. While you may have seen something valuable lost because you tried too hard to cling to it, you have learned how better to choose your battles. You've learned to be more flexible and adaptable. Most importantly, you've learned how to cherish what is important while allowing yourself enough room to make changes so you can keep that thing close without clinging to it.

As you begin to make some of the most important discoveries in your life with the 12 Streams of Income and Fulfillment, there's no underestimating how important this revelation is.

Wall 11: Carrying a Burden

We may not always react to the coming storm by clinging to the rock. We may, instead, try to pick that rock up, hoist it on our backs, and run.

If you've ever tried to carry something heavy uphill, particularly in the rain, you know how exhausting this is. Just as that activity is physically exhausting in life, so too, an emotional burden takes the same toll.

These burdens can be diverse. It may be a friend or relative who constantly needs support or supervision. Maybe you have a sibling that refuses to take care of their kids, so you have to do it, or a friend who constantly relies on recalling the good old days to guilt you into another loan they'll never pay back.

A burden may also involve taking a job you hate that doesn't suit you and that draws from you all your energy and joy in life. But it's a job you can't leave it because you have to provide.

Burdens can be physical, emotional, or financial. They may involve another, many others, or just yourself. Whatever you have to put on your back and carry can be a burden.

Some of these burdens are forced on us, but I don't want to imply every burden is undertaken with ingratitude or without choice. One of the great weights (I would never call it a "burden") of my life was one I chose to carry. When my grandmother got sick and her health began to fail, I chose to provide the care for her. She had been there for me when I needed her, from the time I was two weeks old. When she was called upon to carry me, she never hesitated. Though I must have been a great burden for her, she never complained. She put me on her back, and she carried me to safety. So, when it became clear it was my turn to carry her, I, too, never hesitated.

I made a point to be there for her every day. When I was sick, I found a way to get there. When I was tired, I still got myself up and got to her home. I chose to carry that rock, and I carried it as long as it took. But it was a great weight. So great was it, in fact, I feel it even now, more than three years since she went to heaven.

I carried that weight with joy because it was done with love and it was done by choice. Not every burden is a choice or a joy. Sometimes, it is thrust upon us. No matter how we carry our burden, though, the result is the same. It exhausts us. It wears us down. It makes it so we have no strength left to fight for ourselves. It may leave us permanently a little hobbled. In our effort to preserve what we love most and to show our love, we are left scarred.

Yet, that scar is not something to be ashamed of or to regret. Paul gloried in the "thorn in his flesh." Though there was a time when he had begged God to remove it, he came to see that it drew him closer to God. So, too, you can glory in the ramifications of the burden you carried. Whether you did so by choice or not—whether it brought you joy or not—carrying that burden has shown you have the strength not just to lift yourself but to lift others. It has demonstrated that you have a heart open enough to do more than just succeed for your own sake. You can succeed for others. As we draw closer to your 12 Streams of Income and Fulfillment, you will see how important that element is to not just finding success but feeling fulfilled in that success.

While this wall at first may seem to be full of images of the stress you felt in carrying your burden, you can see them now as pictures that prove one of the great successes of your life. Someone, or something, called upon you for help, and you did not shirk that responsibility. You bent over, put it on your shoulders, and carried it as far as you could.

Wall 12: Acting Out of Character

We often use the expression "out of character" to describe people who just aren't acting like themselves. Whether you've gotten too big a taste of that abundance or you're tied down to your rock, you start behaving in a way that isn't like you. In fact, once you get away from this moment, you can see just like others that the person you were showing the world wasn't you at all. You became somebody else, and even you didn't like you.

This wall is full of items that seem strange to you now you aren't in that moment. The clothes are wrong, the attitude is wrong, the opinions are wrong. Nothing here seems to belong to you.

We can fall out of our character for any number of reasons. Sometimes, as I said above, it's because we've had a bit of very good or very bad fortune. Sometimes, it's because we have met the wrong people, and we try to change who we are to suit them. We meet a romantic partner whom we like but who doesn't like who we are, for instance. Instead of insisting they either love who we are or leave, we try to become someone else to please them.

We may also lose our character in an effort to evade further pain. We're sick of being open, loving, honest, and giving. That seems to leave us vulnerable to those who would take advantage of us. So, we try to become cold, selfish, and judgmental. We wear that personality like a suit of armor, hoping we'll never receive another wound.

In that moment, when we act like someone we're not, we alienate everyone. We alienate those who care about us. "They've changed," they all say. "I hope they change back." At the same time, we alienate ourselves. We don't know who we are, so we feel uncomfortable in ourselves. We're unable to make the right choices because we're not making them from the standpoint of our central values and feelings.

We're probably also alienating those other people we may be trying to impress. Despite our efforts, when we act out of character, we often prove to be bad actors. You can try to be cold, cool, and distant, but if that isn't who you are, you'll only be able to do so much to convince anyone the new you is the real you.

In other words, all you've done in acting out of character is set yourself on the wrong path that isn't true to who you are. You haven't protected yourself at all. You've left yourself exposed, with fewer people there to protect you if something goes wrong.

When I lost my real estate business, I withdrew from others. I acted out of character by cutting myself off from my ambitions. I didn't want to try to succeed again because I was afraid of another huge failure. Instead of being open and filling my life with friends, I tried to act like someone who prefers to keep everyone at a distance. The result, as we already know, was reaching my lowest point, where my life was truly on the line.

This is an isolating moment for anyone, but it's also a great learning experience. After this moment passes, you can see what it took to change your character in this negative way, and you can see where you made the wrong choices in how you reacted to those negative circumstances. At the same time, once you return to yourself, you also get a far better view of who you actually are. Sometimes, you have to lose yourself to appreciate yourself.

You can't protect yourself against losing yourself again until you know who you are in the first place. And it's not until you can protect yourself against who you are not that you can show your true, original character.

That character is the most precious part of this process. Your 12 Streams of Income and Fulfillment are yours alone. They exist only for you. To discover them, though, you'll have to be true to yourself and your journey. There's no room here for success as someone else. We'll need you to be fully you to receive the full wealth at the end of your 12 Streams.

Write out a description of your third set of walls. Detail what happened, how those events have affected you, and whether you have overcome them and moved on.

Wall 9:

_____

_____

_____

_____

Wall 10:

_____

_____

_____

_____

Wall 11:

_____

_____

_____

Wall 12:

_____

_____

_____

Now, write about them not as obstacles that have kept you in a corner but as moments that have allowed you to grow closer to who you are and what you value in your life.

_____

_____

_____

_____

_____

_____

_____

CHAPTER 5

Seeing Your Strength in Your Walls

We now have a blueprint of the home we've built for ourselves. Where once we were stuck in the corner, we're now right at the front door, ready to use the keys we'll discover in the next section to get out into the world and find our 12 Streams of Income and Fulfillment.

Before we leave here, though, I want to take a moment to look back at all that we've covered. It can be tempting, after reviewing all the difficulties we've experienced in life, to shrug it all off and say, "good riddance."

While I've pointed out throughout that these events are in fact positive in the longer run, it can still be difficult to digest that point. We are so intensely connected to those tough moments the pain we still feel can blind us to the value of our experience.

These twelve events were things we never wanted to go through. If any of us had access to a time machine, many of these walls would get demolished and never get rebuilt. After all, who wants to live through pain? Who wants to make sacrifices? Who wants to reach such brutal, humiliating, and dark low points?

No one, of course, and yet, success can't happen if we don't first experience those difficulties. David would never have made much of a king if he hadn't known what it was like to love and yet be betrayed by Saul. He had to lose his closest friend and his son. He had to make awful mistakes, including murder. It couldn't have been otherwise. If he'd sailed through life, he wouldn't have had the wisdom it took to build his dynasty.

In other words, these walls may feel like they've been blocking you in, when what they've really been doing is laying the foundation for the strength you now possess to succeed. These experiences were tough, but they are what have made you strong enough to achieve your 12 Streams of Income and Fulfillment.

The good things in life are joyous, but they don't teach us much. I'm sure there are some people out there who have known only joy in life, but I don't think they've learned much from their experience, and I doubt they're much older than three. By the time they're five, they'll have fallen off the bike at least once. They'll have learned a little about pain, and failure, and disappointment. But they'll also have learned how to get back up and get back on that bike.

We need these walls to give us the strength to be who we need to be and to achieve what we need to achieve. None of those situations may have felt very good when you were going through them (if you have even completely gotten through them), but they are what has prepared you for right now. They are what have given you the strength to make it through this book and to implement the advice you'll find here.

There's no shame in running into any of these foundational walls. The only shame is continuing to wander blindly into the same situations.

Now you have this foundation, now you have these walls, your entrance to the 12 Streams is protected. You've got the infrastructure in place to get where you are going. Now, those 12 Streams can flow in.

Proverbs tells us:

So shall the knowledge of wisdom be to your soul;
If you have found it, there is a prospect,
And your hope will not be cut off.

In other words, above all else, get wisdom because that is the key to your success. That's what you've accomplished with these walls. Whether you've built up all twelve of them or you've only experienced three or four, each one you've erected has provided you with the wisdom you require to move beyond the limitations your life has experienced so far and to expand your prospects, so that you can discover your true and full potential.

These walls, then, aren't just foundations that you built. *They've* built *you*, too. You thought when you went through these situations that they were there to destroy you, to tear you down. Really, they were building you up, so that you would be strong enough for this very moment.

SECTION II.

THE 5 KEYS

OF TRUST

CHAPTER 6

Standing in Front of a Close Door

We left off standing in the front room of this magnificent building we have constructed out of all the difficulties we've faced in our lives. The sun is streaming in through our front windows and a dark, confining space has turned into a castle of strength before our eyes. We've left behind the years where we saw this place as a prison. Now, we can see it for what it is: our stronghold, our source of wisdom. These walls are tough and sturdy, but they're not designed to keep us in, they're designed to protect us against all the struggles we have to face in our future. They aren't meant to trap you within; they are meant to keep new struggles from knocking you over again.

We can be grateful for those walls now, but that doesn't mean we want to spend any more time in here. After all, we can now see through our front windows not just the warm and inviting sun but, in the distance, those twelve lush, flowing Streams of Income and Fulfillment. Understandably, then, we don't want to waste any more time appreciating walls we know so well already. Instead, we want to get out as quickly as we possibly can.

But how do we go about it? We could try to cut a hole in one of these sturdy walls, but we have plenty of experience to prove going through walls (instead of using them for support) can be a painful and ineffective solution to our problem. We could break a window, but that also seems a rather violent and potentially painful way to get outside. It's also a waste of effort, particularly as there's a door right in front of us, perfectly capable of leading us out to the outdoors and all our opportunities.

However, when we walk up and try the door knob, we discover there's a new problem: the door's locked. Worse, it isn't just locked once. It's got five locks on it, and a quick look at each shows that each of them requires a different key. Giving the door a shake, you can tell it is not going to budge without first using the keys.

The old you would have been discouraged by this fact. The old you would have moped back to your corner in the back room. Or, maybe, you would have just banged on the door and tried to break it down, only to find yourself bruised and disheartened when the door wouldn't yield. Either way, the old you would have decided you really were trapped; you would have been worse off than before we started this process.

Thankfully, that old you is gone now. You're stronger and wiser now you've made the journey through this home. Instead of acting rashly, or giving up quickly, you know there's a better way to go about things. Give the room a quick look-around. Just as you previously misunderstood the meaning of the walls around you, you may also have forgotten to look closely at the objects around you. There's a table, a sofa, a mantel, a bookshelf. There are objects everywhere, now that you take a moment to look.

Keep scanning the furniture, the walls, and the floor. Do you see something gleaming and metallic? Pick it up. Here we are, then, a set of keys, five in total, just like the locks.

All we have to do now is to figure out which key fits which lock. Take a closer look at the keys. Each one as one big word etched into it—"Trust"—and then more information scribbled in smaller letters below.

To fit the right key to the right lock, then, we've got to understand just what "trust" means for each key. That's the only way to progress, the only way to further our journey. We've got to understand trust to move beyond this world of our old experiences and progress into the present moment of our coming success.

Write your definition of "trust." What do you trust in life? Do you trust yourself?

CHAPTER 7

The 5 Keys to Trust

When we examined our 12 Walls of Support, we looked primarily at your past. In that first section, we reviewed the events that have made you tough, strong, wise, and capable. Those walls have included events that happened to you and choices you made because of those events. The moments were awful at the time, but they brought you to this present moment, where you now stand on the doorway to success.

The keys are different. Here, we're not talking about experiences and events in the past; we're talking about how you view yourself and your world today. Going through all those tough times probably had a lot of major effects on you, but one of the most common is that they sap you of all your self-confidence, self-belief, and self-motivation.

Why do people who fall down stay down? Because they feel like they can't trust themselves to stand up again. They're sure they'll fall or get knocked down again. They don't stay down because they like it down on the ground; they stay down because they don't believe things are going to get any better if they stand back up again.

Looked at another way; the only way to transform the trauma of your 12 Walls into strength is to heal the self-trust within you that is broken.

You have to learn not just to see the strength you've encountered and the strength you've overcome, but to trust the strength that such events have built within you.

To do that, you may have guessed, you'll need to understand these five keys. Each key targets a different aspect of trust you'll have to reveal, recognize, and recover in order to move beyond the door that's currently blocking you from all your future prosperity.

Let's not waste any more time justifying the need for these keys. You know yourself that you could use more belief in yourself. If you already knew you could achieve all your dreams, you'd be swimming in those streams today. You need this, and you can have this, so long as you take hold of the keys I'm giving you.

Key 1: Trust Who You Are

This kind of trust sounds elementary, but most of us don't really examine what the words actually mean.

"Yeah, Jack, I trust myself. Who else am I going to trust?"

The thing is, though, you probably don't. I'm going to guess when you really think about it honestly, you don't particularly like or trust yourself that much at all.

That's fine. That's natural. As human beings, it's part of our nature not to see what's working but to see what's broken.

Think about it this way: when you look in the mirror, do you see all the parts of you that look good and function properly, or do you see the problems?

There's a little too much weight around your middle. Something's sagging, something's dropping. There's a new wrinkle around your eyes or lips. Your teeth could be whiter. Your hair could look better. You could stand up straighter.

You should lift weights. You should run. You should diet. You should get a haircut. You should get a manicure. You should buy nicer clothes. You should get more stylish shoes.

I could go on. I know you do. And that's only the physical stuff. Every time you think of yourself, you feel down about yourself.

Again, this is normal. As a species, we're perfectionists. If you just looked in the mirror every day and said, "Good enough," you'd never get anywhere. You're not satisfied with your life, and there's a reason for that. You know it's not all "good enough."

Here's the thing, though. You may be right that life isn't "good enough" yet, but you certainly are. You need to learn to see yourself not as a collection of faults, mistakes, and imperfections, but as a collection of powerful and successful features.

Sure, you're not as tall as you would like to be. You're not as thin as you could be. You're not as beautiful as some models. You're not as clever as some comedians. You're not as smart as some astrophysicists. But you don't need to be. You are precisely what you need to be to achieve your 12 Streams of Income and Fulfillment.

I'm the last person to put myself up as the ideal of perfection. I have my faults, and I can give you a long list of people who could name them all in detail. My success didn't come because I suddenly became the smartest, strongest, most innovative person on the planet. It came because I recognized that the skills I had, the strengths I had, the wisdom I had was perfect for the 12 Streams of Income and Fulfillment that existed in the world just for me. *My* strengths matched the needs for *my* 12 Streams.

I had to trust that I was good enough for the success that I wanted to come my way.

There's no way around this realization. You are who you are, and that's the only person you're ever going to be. You can't be anybody else. You can pretend to be someone else. You can mimic someone else. You're still going to be you.

You're the only person you brought to the party. So, if you want to dance, you've got to get comfortable with your dance partner: *you.*

You have to be comfortable with the person you are. You have to be able to look in the mirror and see the whole person—the strengths and the flaws—and trust that that person is not just "good enough" but the exact right person to achieve the dreams you have. You have to trust that person to make the right decisions and to look after you as you make your journey to your individual streams.

It's only once you trust yourself that the world can come to trust you and open up its opportunities to you. After all, we can't ask others to trust us if we don't trust ourselves.

Imagine walking into a board room to sell your most brilliant idea. If you are filled with self-doubt, you're going to speak quietly, constantly apologizing for every little mistake, refusing to make eye contact, and looking for the quickest way possible out of the room. Does that sound like the kind of person important, wealthy businesspeople want to do business with?

Alternatively, if you trust yourself, and trust that you are the right person to make this pitch, you'll walk in confident, charming, amusing, and speak with the authority to earn these people's trust.

The first version of you gets a quick rejection and a quick exit. The second version gets the deal.

I couldn't sell a single house if I didn't believe I had within me all the right skills to know this was the right property for this buyer, this was the right price, and I could make them see that. If I didn't wake up and see in the mirror a man designed to be a successful real estate broker, I couldn't do it. I know that's true because in the years I didn't wake up and see that man in the mirror, I couldn't do the work. It was a long journey back to trusting who I was.

Developing this trust in who you are, is a skill in itself. In fact, it's the key skill required in transforming the experiences of those walls into the internal strength you need to move forward in your journey. To develop this skill, you have to absorb the main lesson of the last section: everything you've done in your life was building you up to be this very person at this very moment. And that person is the perfect person to achieve the goals life has in store for you.

That person isn't perfect, but those imperfections are part of your strength. Remember, Paul thanked God he was afflicted by the thorn in his flesh. That thorn wasn't actually a weakness; it was his great strength. But it was only his great strength because he had trust in himself and in God.

Paul realized this when the Lord told him, "My strength is made perfect in weakness." Paul wasn't strong because he overcame his thorn; he was strong *because of* the thorn.

You see those wrinkles in the mirror? They're a sign of your wisdom scrawled across your face. You see that hunch in your shoulders? That's a sign you've bent your back learning to work hard. Your stutter? It's the feature that lets you better consider your words (another Key we'll soon learn about). Your history of depression or anxiety? That's the unique perspective that allows you to reach out to the world in a new, stronger, more compassionate way. Your quick temper? That reveals your passion that can be directed toward your goals.

Whatever your thorn, whatever the faults you see, those are really your strengths in disguise. But to harness those strengths, you have to get beyond being self-critical and become self-trusting.

All that you have been through, those events weren't designed to make you lose faith in yourself. Instead, they were meant to give you a new education, to better your understanding of yourself. The walls in this home have taught you how powerful you are, how capable you are to go through hardship and make tough choices. Your life has forced you to trust yourself over and over again. It has forced you to rely on yourself. It's time to repay that experience and learn the lesson it's been teaching you: you've got this. Relax, because you're at the wheel, and you're more than capable of getting where you're going.

Look, you are the *only you* you are ever going to have. So, stop looking for what's wrong with *you* and trust that *you* are the right person for the tasks ahead.

Key 2: Trust What You Know

A woman named Michelle once came into my office with a question she needed advice on. She owned a piece of potentially lucrative property she hadn't been using. While it was sitting around empty, she allowed a friend to stay there on a temporary basis. Now, an investment opportunity had arisen, and she wanted to sell the property. But what should she do about the friend?

The friend had overstayed the temporary time she was meant to remain in the home, and she'd clearly settled in with an eye on staying indefinitely. That left Michelle in a bind. Selling the home was good for Michelle's future plans but meant betraying her friend. Not selling the home kept the friendship strong and allowed her to feel loyal, but it also meant she had to stop dead in her plans for her own life.

I helped Michelle talk out all of her potential options. At the end of our conversation, though, she asked, "But, Jack, what should I do?"

I told her outright that only she could make that decision, and she would have to own that choice. I couldn't tell her whether the friendship or her upcoming opportunities were more important. Only she could do that. If it were my home, I would make certain decisions, but that would be *my* life, *my* friend, and *my* business opportunities. That would be *my* decision.

In the end, I discovered she wasn't looking for advice; she was looking for someone to pass the responsibility to. She didn't trust enough in her own judgment.

Michelle's situation isn't a rare one. Most of us struggle with this in life. In fact, one of the big reasons people struggle to trust who they are and discover success is that they just don't believe they're smart enough to handle the tough calls.

From the outside, success can look like something only the most brilliant will ever achieve. There's a reason we feel that way: it's built into our culture. We have a bit of a worship problem with successful people. We tend to see them as impossibly, untouchably clever, geniuses that were simply born with all the best ideas.

There's some truth in that in some cases, but we do ourselves a huge disservice assuming that the formula is as simple as a high IQ equals success or an expensive education equals success. Those things can be a nice boon if everything else is in place, but they won't make you a success. In fact, they sometimes don't matter at all.

Bill Gates, Steve Jobs, Paul Allen, Michael Dell, Larry Ellison, and Ted Turner are all college dropouts. They're also all billionaires. Some of the richest people in the history of America, including John D. Rockefeller and Henry Ford, never saw the inside of a college classroom. Ford didn't even finish high school. Neither did Dave Thomas, the founder of Wendy's.

In all those cases, education wasn't the key to their success. So what did make a difference? Trusting they knew enough to make the right decisions in their lives and their businesses.

Trusting that you know enough is crucial to getting beyond the experience of the building we're in and getting on the path toward our 12 Streams of Income and Fulfillment. You have to be able to know you've got the wisdom to make the right choices. Otherwise, you'll either end up letting someone else make the choice or make no choice at all when the big decisions come along.

I don't blame anyone for struggling with these issues. No one wants to make tough decisions or be the bad guy. Unfortunately, life puts us in these situations, and we have to be ready to trust in ourselves, our instincts, and our experiences. Going to Harvard wouldn't have made Michelle's choice any easier. Taking more classes or reading more books or getting an internship wouldn't have given her the answer.

In the end, she had the answer all along: she knew she couldn't pass up on her business opportunities, and she knew she had to tell the friend it was time to go. She *knew* the right answer; she just didn't trust herself to make it. She came to me so I could make it for her because she thought I was some kind of expert on the matter due to my experience in real estate.

I told her, like I'm telling you, that I have the right experience for my life. She's got the right experience for hers. She knew the answer. Her own wisdom told it to her. She just needed to trust herself and make the call.

Everything we've done so far, every place we've been, everything we've worked on, everything we've been a part of, is all gone into the construction of our personal library of experience and knowledge. That library is more than enough to allow you to make the big decisions in your life, whether they're personal or professional. Don't listen to that voice in your head that tells you someone else is smarter and better able to make that choice. You may be surprised to find out that the people who always claim to be the smartest—the ones always most eager to shout out how much they know—are often the ones who know the least and are the least wise and useful. This isn't just experience talking (though I've known plenty of blowhards in my time), it's science.

This phenomenon is called the Dunning–Kruger effect. It states that those who know very little tend to think they know a lot, while those who know a lot tend to think they are extremely ignorant. The ignorant assume they're experts; the experts are sure they don't know anything at all.

Put that knowledge into the context of your own life. The guy who's always telling you how to navigate every problem in your life, and his life, and someone else's life? That guy probably knows the least about solving those problems. Meanwhile, you, who think you are simply too ignorant about the world to solve your own problems, what does the Dunning–Kruger effect say about you?

It says you know plenty. You could solve all your problems, if you would just give yourself the credit you deserve. Your experiences have led you to know what you need to know today. You know enough to know what you need to do at this moment in your life.

That doesn't mean you know everything. I don't want you to get a big head and think every problem is a cinch and all you've got to do is go with your initial gut reaction and move forward thoughtlessly. By all means, you should solicit advice from those you respect. You should seek council from the wise, the experienced, and the holy. Speak to business colleagues about taking on new business opportunities. Speak to your pastor about relationships and faith. Speak to family about a potential move.

But when it comes down to it, the last word on this subject should be yours, and it should be delivered with confidence because you've got the wisdom within you to find the answer.

Tell yourself: "What I know, I know. What I don't know, I'll learn when I need to."

You still have a lot of learning ahead, but the problems of today can be solved with the wisdom of today. If you can't make the decision this second, find the little pieces of missing understanding, and then make it.

I learned something a long time ago. You want to make your decisions quickly and then change them as you go. If you just let a decision sit, it becomes bigger and bigger. It becomes so big in your mind, it soon feels unsolvable. Where you might have known the moment—you knew right away if you should take that new job or not—by sitting on the choice for a week, you've managed to overthink yourself into an impossible corner.

If your experience and your internal wisdom told you to take the job, take it. If not, don't. Other jobs will come along if this one doesn't work out.

That doesn't mean you'll never make a mistake, but the mistakes you'll make will be minimal compared to all the lost opportunities you let pass by while you thought too long.

Because Michelle finally made her decision, she was able to sell her property and help her friend find another place to stay. If she'd waited much longer, she would have missed out on the investment opportunity that afforded her the income to help her friend as well. Then, she would have been sitting around, her property still unsold, her own financial position worse off, her friend no closer to moving on with her life, and Michelle now living with a sense of resentment toward that friend. That, clearly, would have been a far bigger mistake.

We should have taken a valuable lesson from our 12 Walls of Support: whenever we make a mistake, just go back and see what happened.

Put the plane back together and find out why it crashed. You've walked away from a lot of plane crashes already. You'll walk away from this one too, if it proves to be a mistake. As long as you're learning, it wasn't a mistake, it was an experience.

And, again, it's far less likely to be a mistake, since you already have the experience to make the right call and make it quickly.

Key 3: Trust Where You're Going

Speaking of indecision, people often struggle to find success precisely because they don't trust their internal compass to point them in the right direction.

I don't know how many people have come up to me at some point and said something like, "I'm thinking about maybe moving to California and see what happens."

Let's unpack that a bit. Thinking about it? Maybe moving? See what happens? Everything about that statement suggests they're setting themselves up for failure and disappointment.

If you want to move to California, start planning, save up, and go. Go with a plan in mind for what you're going to do once you get out there. Develop a strategy and implement it.

You don't want to waste your time "maybe" "thinking about" it. You don't want to put in all that effort to get out to one of the most expensive parts of the country just to "see what happens." When you make a big decision to change the course of your life, you want to know where you're going and what you're going to do.

We have to have more trust in the direction we take. Move to California but move there with purpose. Ask yourself, "Why do I want to move to California?" I'm not going to tell you there should be one set answer, but there should be an answer. It can be as simple as, "I love the climate, and that's where I see myself happiest." Or, "I have friends out there, and I feel that's where I'll find the community to support me." Or, "There are far more business opportunities for what I do out there." It can be anything, but it has to be something. And it has to be something concrete enough to build a life on. Success is not a place, success is you. California, in and of itself, isn't going to make you a success. California may help you discover that success. It can be a tool you use to discover success and fulfillment. But, like education, it is just a tool. It isn't a guarantee.

Knowing why you're going in a certain direction in life is crucial. Equally crucial is trusting you've made the right choice and committing to it once the choice is made.

All those people I've known who "tried" California? A lot of them came back not too long afterward, a little discouraged, a lot poorer, and feeling completely directionless. Why did they come back? Most of the time, it's because of two things. First, they didn't do the research to make sure success was available to them out in California. Second, they didn't commit to their decision.

If you don't have that trust in your direction, it's very easy to end up moving backward, sideways, cross-ways, and every other direction but forward. It's just too easy to back out of a big moment when it arrives.

If you choose to pursue a big project like moving from the East Coast to California, you are inevitably going to have some setbacks. The jobs will perhaps be harder to come by than you expected. The rent will be higher than you wanted to pay. Your friends will be less available to support you than you counted on.

For those who aren't committed to their path, those setbacks are a huge rebuke to their choices. Instead of doubling down and showing their internal strength to overcome a new difficulty, they retreat. They run away. They fail.

That's because they weren't completely sold on California. They weren't willing to go all in on it. They weren't sure they could trust that direction.

You may not realize it, sitting down and reading this book right now, but you know by now what you want. You know the right direction you want to drive your life. You've been through enough, you've gained enough wisdom, that the answers are within you.

We live in a time where everyone suffers from FOMO: Fear of Missing Out. There will always be roads not taken, possibilities never to be explored. And in the modern Facebook-saturated world, you'll be more aware of those choices lost to history than in previous times.

You will get out to California and discover someone else has moved to Miami, and they're looking all kinds of happy and successful. Someone else moved to Alaska, and man, does that place look beautiful. Another friend just settled in the Midwest and the prices are so affordable!

In some alternative universe, any of those people could be you. But in this world, they aren't you. You're in California. Why are you in California? Because that was the right choice for you. Trust in your instincts for the direction you need to go. You have within you a compass that is going to point where you need to be. Take a moment to see what it is telling you, then commit—fully—to going in that direction.

That direction may not always be the easiest. There will be sacrifices required, just as there are benefits attained along the way. There will always be alternative paths that you didn't take somewhere behind you.

None of that matters. What matters is that your compass is pointing toward *your* 12 Streams of Income and Fulfillment. It's not pointing toward your friend's streams in Colorado or Spain. It's not pointing toward some celebrity's streams in Cancun. It's taking you to your streams—your individual, personal streams. Your goal in life isn't to take every path; it's to take your path. And once you find that path, to stick to it.

Use your experience to know where you are, where you want to be, and how you're going to get there.

Then, get walking.

Key 4: Trust What You Say

It's an old-fashioned idea, but it remains true today: we live by our word. What we say has consequences. If we present ourselves in an honest and direct way, we will be respected for our word. If we deceive, mislead, overpromise, or otherwise fail to display the truth behind our words, we'll eventually pay for it.

So, we have to be truthful.

This is more complicated—and more difficult—than we may initially think. After all, most of us probably think of ourselves as truthful. And in simple situations without a lot of downside, we probably are. It's those less straightforward situations in which there are potential difficulties to telling the truth that we run into trouble.

"Are you happy in this job?" your boss asks you. How are you going to respond? Will you be truthful and say, "No, and here's why"? Or will you demure and hide the truth as well as possible?

That example shows an important fact about telling lies: hiding the truth isn't always malicious. It isn't always done by the thoughtless or the cruel. We all tell lies, more often than we might believe. This goes all the way back to childhood. We all had our missing cookie episodes. "Did you take the cookie from the cookie jar?" an adult asks. And we say, "No." We insist we didn't do it. We play at being offended they even asked. We plead for them to believe us. All while the crumbs are all over our shirt.

If it isn't cookies, it's the broken lamp. If it isn't the broken lamp, it's the stain on the carpet or the crayons on the wall. No matter the circumstance, our childish instinct was the same: deny, deny, deny, even when the evidence is clear.

Why didn't we just admit it?

We didn't admit it because something inside us told us it was better to take the chance to avoid the risk of punishment. We didn't want to disappoint or anger someone we cared about, and we didn't want to face the consequences for our choices.

After all, who wants to be grounded? Who wants to miss out on playing outside with friends? Who wants to see that look of rebuke from someone we respect?

So, we develop a habit of lying in the tough moments, and by the time we reach adulthood, it's so deeply within us, we hardly notice when we do it anymore.

"Will you come to this event?" a colleague asks. "Sure," we say, even as we begin to think about excuses for why we missed it. The truth is we don't want to go. We have other plans or just need some time alone to reenergize. The person in front of us would probably accept those true reasons. Yet, here we are, lying all the same.

In these day-to-day interactions, this can seem harmless. After all, it's easier for us, and the results are the same, so what does it matter?

I'll leave that to the Bible: "Faith comes by hearing."

If you hear yourself lying and getting away with it, you'll begin to have faith that you can always get away with lying, instead of having faith in the truth. At the same time, as others hear you regularly misstate the truth, they'll come to see you as less reliable.

This doesn't have to be a conscious decision. They may think you're still a great person, fun, capable, and much else. But on some level, they'll know they can't expect you to be decisive and to live by your word. They won't believe you when you say, "This is where I'm going, and I'm going to get there."

When we're trying to lead ourselves in a new direction, into the new, unexplored territory where our 12 Streams of Income and Fulfillment reside, we have to be able to speak clearly and truthfully and be believed.

To do that, we have to start telling the truth, even when there are consequences. Sometimes, the truth costs you something. You'll get punished for eating that cookie. You might get a nasty look when you say you just don't want to go to that party, that you'd rather spend the evening reading. But telling the truth is a lesson we have to learn because then we know we can trust what we say. And others will know it, too.

I don't mean to tell you to be blunt and rude. You don't have to answer how you feel about your job by listing off every minor problem you have with the management, the job, the pay, and everything else. But if your boss asks if you like the job, you should be truthful. Tell him, "No." Be polite, but be direct. That may be the way forward in resolving your problems with the position. Lying just secures the status quo. Lying won't make anything better.

Can you imagine what your life would be like if everyone knew that what came out of your mouth was the truth? The truth, the whole truth, and nothing but the truth?

You would teach people to believe you, every time you speak. If you said you'd be somewhere, they'd know you'd be there. They'd plan for you to be there. They'd have your hors d'oeuvres and your drink sitting there waiting for when you show up. If you said you were going to make a success of yourself in one year, they'd know you were going to do it, and they'd want to get involved.

Suddenly, "I need some investment for my new business," becomes an opportunity for everyone instead of a moment when they think of ways to lie to you about why they can't help out. Now, they know when you say this business is going to work, that you know what you're talking about.

As an added bonus, you'll also cut through most of the falsehoods that exist around you. When we are honest and direct, we encourage that from others. If you tell someone you won't be at an event because you just don't feel up to it, they'll give you the same kind of courtesy next time the invitation runs the other way around. As your reputation grows for honesty, more honesty will come from those around you.

Most importantly, though, it won't just be others who trust in your words, it'll be you. This is so important because, after all, the person we lie to most often is ourselves. These lies come in many forms. We've already seen some, where we lie to ourselves that we are stupid and talentless and incapable of success when we look in the mirror. We also lie about our past, making it worse than it was or better than it was, depending on how we're feeling. We lie about why we're doing what we're doing. Sometimes, we lie so hard, we convince ourselves we really *did* want to go to that party, it's just something came up. We'll lie even when we made the point of planning something to conflict with the party.

If you're so tied up with internal lies, how on earth can you make yourself believe that you really are on the doorstep of your 12 Streams of Income and Fulfillment? You can't. You've got to know that you are telling yourself the truth, and that you can take that truth to the bank.

Over a lifetime, we have become experts at telling a lie over and over to ourselves. We'll tell the same lie so many times, we will believe it. That can be a very dangerous habit. If we lie and tell ourselves over and over again that we are doomed to failure, we will eventually believe this isn't just true, it is a whole and unchangeable truth, as true as the fact you're reading this book right now. This is the sort of thing that put us in that corner in the first place. We lied and said there was no way out. We lied and said we couldn't get out of the corner, we couldn't get out of the room, or we couldn't get out of the house. We lied and said everyone else has 12 Streams of Income and Fulfillment, but we don't have any.

At that point, you begin to live the lie. You have told yourself so often you're a loser, you act like a loser. You quit jobs that could have led to good careers. Why? Because you're a loser. You cut off contact with your friends when they want to help. Why? Because you're a loser.

You aren't a loser, though. You're just a liar. A liar who specializes in the worst kinds of lies: the ones you tell to yourself.

We already know at this point that you are capable, strong, and wise enough to achieve your dreams. We know that, but now you have to believe it. You've got to believe it by telling yourself and knowing you're telling the truth.

And to know you're telling the truth, you have to let your truth flow through your life. You have to be swimming in truth if you want to swim in those 12 streams.

That means you've got to learn to say "no" when the answer is "no." My grandmother, a wise woman, used to say, "Let your yes be yes, and let your no be no." She also said, "Sometimes no is the right answer."

When the moment requires a "no," embrace that "no." Don't hint it, don't misdirect, and don't lie. Just say, "No." You may be surprised how well people take such a direct truth, even when it isn't the answer they want.

Nothing breeds faster and more plentifully than an untruth. When we start telling them, they quickly fill up all the space around us, until we can't tell the few truths left from all the untruths. These untruths work to block our opportunities and potential. They close off the paths forward that can lead to our 12 Streams of Income and Fulfillment. Instead of letting every "no" become a "yes," let the truth protect you and clear the way forward.

Remember, in this world, there are always people watching. When they watch us, do they see an honest person on the path toward their success? Or do they see the lies, the liar, and the failure we've built over our lifetimes?

Trust in yourself and ensure others can trust you by speaking truth.

Once you know your truth, you can show it to others, and they will know they can trust it. When your truth is the key to your success, you know you don't want to hedge on this.

Conversely, we already know we can doubt ourselves because we feel we don't have enough (or the right kind) of experiences. You may have read through the 12 Walls of Support and said, "Man, I haven't been through any of this." Which then makes you think: "I must not be ready."

I can tell you right now, though, you're ready. How do I know? Because you're here.

There's no such thing as being too old or too young to achieve your 12 Streams of Income and Fulfillment. Stevie Wonder was a success from age 11 when he signed to Motown Records. Ray Kroc didn't become invested in the burger place that would become McDonald's until he was in his fifties. Mark Zuckerberg launched Facebook when he was 19. Colonel Sanders got into the chicken industry at 62. There's no right time for success. The right time is special to you, and the moment for you is now.

So, be comfortable in your skin, in your place, in your moment. You are the right person for the job, with the right skills, heading in the right direction, with the truth on your side, and this is just the moment to burst through the door and head for your success.

That success can take whatever shape you dream, even, or perhaps particularly, an unexpected one. When I was in school and they'd have reading time, I'd slink down in my chair, trying to avoid getting called on. I made every effort to avoid reading the books assigned in class. I showed no interest in writing essays. I did all sorts of work when I got out of school, but none of it involved a lot of writing. So, who would have thought, looking at that young man, "That boy's going to be an author"?

And yet, now the moment has come, and that's precisely what I turned out to be. Now that I've finally followed the path set forth for me in revelation to its conclusion, I've discovered that that is just what this stream had put in store for me.

When the time was right, the path was revealed. My path led me here, to this book. Where is your path going to lead you?

Outline your issues with trust. What events led you to break trust in yourself and others?

_____

_____

_____

_____

_____

_____

_____

_____

Write out the reasons you deserve trust from others, but especially, from yourself. Think of the qualities in your personality and moments in your past that you proved you were capable of achieving as you dream of.

_____

_____

_____

_____

_____

_____

_____

_____

_____

Are you known as someone whose word can be trusted? If not, what can you do, starting today, to improve people's trust in your word?

_____

_____

_____

_____

_____

_____

_____

Look around you; consider your whole life in this moment. Write about the ways you know that this is the right moment to pursue your 12 Streams. Write about the signs that show you are on the right path for your success.

CHAPTER 8

Opening the Door to Your Possibilities

With all five keys inserted into their individual locks, it's now time to enjoy the turn of each as the door slowly becomes unlatched and access to the fresh air and bright skies of your future becomes possible.

Before we step outside and take our first steps into the world—as we will in the next section—I want to take a moment to discuss a little further what these keys have done for you.

After all, most books will tell you that you need to have a little more self-confidence if you want to be a success. Why were these keys so important? Why couldn't we just skip over this with a quick line about "believing in yourself," bust the door down, and get going?

There's a reason this revelation focused so much on these five keys. Nothing in life can go very far without a lot of trust. There has to be trust between people in order to work together. There has to be trust in the world to know it's worth stepping outside your door every day to go to work. There has to be trust in the system that there's a way to make a success of yourself. There has to be trust in God that the world is ultimately just and right. And, as we now know, there has to be trust within ourselves that we are capable of achieving what we dream.

I know a lot about what it means to lose trust in your life. Part of what led me to my lowest moment was a loss of trust. I didn't believe that I could get myself out of the position I was in. I didn't trust in my abilities. I didn't trust enough in my family that they would find a way to support me. I wasn't able to trust enough in my church to shelter my broken spirit. And my trust in the world, in the idea of success, that was completely and truly shattered.

I know a lot of you out there are feeling the same way I did. If you aren't feeling it now, you've felt it in the past. The love of your life ran away, and you are hurting where that trust used to be. The dream job went to someone else, and now you're feeling jealousy instead of trust. The bills keep piling up, and you've got too many worries about where the money's going to come from to spend much energy on building up trust that the answer is around the corner.

We all, every one of us, suffer from too little trust in this world of ours. It's difficult to keep trust alive. Life can be full of bad news, disappointments, setbacks, and compromises. That's not a great recipe for a thriving sense of trust in ourselves, others, and the world around us.

What these keys have done, then, is make you and me analyze where our trust is lacking. Often, we don't realize that what we're suffering from is actually a lack of trust. When we feel lonely after a year of nursing that broken heart, we blame ourselves for being unlovable or failing to put ourselves out there again. Our real problem is that we haven't repaired the trust that is broken within ourselves. We aren't able to trust that there's another person out there for us, who will love us right. When I couldn't get myself out the door to try again after my real estate business collapsed, my primary obstacle wasn't the lack of opportunities; it was a lack of trust that those opportunities would lead me back to success again. When we feel there are too many obligations being put on us, the obligations are a great weight. But often, we don't take the opportunities that arise to decrease that weight because we lack trust in others. We don't trust them to take some of the weight from us to ease our burden.

The self-analyzing of the 5 Keys of Trust can help us grow into the knowledge of where we are and who we are while clarifying where our lack of trust has been holding us back. I can't emphasize enough how important trust is in life. We put our trust in every step we take. Literally, every step we take involves trust that our feet will catch us before we fall. Every time we cross a street, every time we take a bite of food, every time we close our eyes, we are trusting that the next moment will not lead to a tragedy. We won't be hit by a car, we won't choke; we will wake up again. We're trusting every moment to lead to another.

Trust is that intimately connected to our existence. If we can't get from one bite of food to the next without trust, how can we get from this moment to our 12 Streams of Income and Fulfillment without far more trust?

Trust has to be central to our existence. It's the only way to take the experiences of the 12 Walls of Support and turn them into strength instead of regret. It's the only way to bridge the gap between those actions of the past and our perspective of the present we will explore ahead in the 7 Steps to Your Potential.

The revelations in this section are bound to lead to some serious changes. You're going to see yourself differently. You're going to see others differently, too. You'll start to see where you have failed to trust yourself, and as you begin to trust yourself again, you'll see changes in how you behave and how you approach situations. Your conversation will probably change as well. You're sure to become more mindful over what you say, who you are, and who you are developing into.

Embrace this change. Trust in the change. As you reach out, grasp the doorknob, and turn it, pulling the door open and feeling the direct sunlight and the breeze for the first time in years, remember to take a moment, close your eyes, and just trust that, finally, you're moving in the right direction.

SECTION III.

THE 7 STEPS TO

YOUR POTENTIAL

CHAPTER 9

Moving Forward, Into Your Present

Y ou've opened the door on your present now. Gone are the hard-luck, tough-learning days of your past. In the distance, in a beautiful and lush valley, you can now clearly make out your 12 Streams of Income and Fulfillment flowing joyously and invitingly. However, there's a steep hill that runs straight from your front door down to where the streams are.

To get beyond your doorstep, you're going to have to find a way down. With such a steep hill, it'd be easy to settle for what you've got right now. After all, the sun is shining, the breeze is refreshing, and the view is spectacular. You've made peace with your past, and while you may not have accomplished much, you've become more comfortable with who you are. You're more willing to trust and be trusted. That's a lot of progress, even if it doesn't quite get you where you want to be.

And there are always risks when trying to get beyond your porch. Every step beyond this safe point could lead to a fall. Where you are now is not as fulfilling as you'd like, but moving forward means the chance of scrapes, bruises, and broken bones. From this moment forward, you're not just coming to terms with what has happened; you're making real, concrete progress toward the meaning of your life. That's a scary effort to undertake.

After all, you're not used to this kind of climbing. You've spent a long time—years, maybe decades—just trying to survive in that corner in the back room in your home. You've been living in the shadows and doubt of your past. You've hidden yourself from your ambitions and hopes. You've tried to avoid really living in the moment because you never liked the moment.

To find the courage and skill to move now, living fully in the present, with your 12 Streams constantly in mind, you're going to need to learn how to walk again, step by step.

The first two sections of this book allowed you to become comfortable with where you came from. Your past wasn't hardship just for hardship's sake. You were learning the wisdom you would need to discover your ultimate success. You need to keep all those lessons with you, but up to this point, we've failed to do more than just draw lessons from the past. You now need to learn how to live in your day-to-day life.

This isn't easy. Most of us have spent most of our time either dreaming of a brighter future or dwelling on the best and worst of our past. Life has been something that just sort of happens around us while our minds have been elsewhere. As John Lennon once sang, "Life is what happens to you when you're busy making other plans." For a long time, we've been making plans or reliving our past while life passed us by. We didn't focus on our actions in the moment. We did what we had to do, just to get by, but when we could, we would go on autopilot.

This problem is even more common today than it was in the past. These days, our whole lives are taken up with distractions that keep us from a committed focus on living and moving toward our goals. When we get up, we don't take in the moment and prepare for the day, we look at our phones. We check social media, check our email, and zone out on our bright screens. On our way to work, we encounter advertisements everywhere we look. They're on the bus and the train and on the billboards on the side of the road. At work, there's always time to surf the Internet instead of completing projects. Or we waste our time gossiping instead of investing it in our jobs or prospects. When we get home, it's straight to the TV, where we spend our evenings watching show after show after show. Then, it's back to bed, where our main companion is once again our phones.

There's not a single moment in our lives that is guaranteed to be free from distractions. These distractions aren't bad in themselves—we all need some time to relax and take it easy. However, they do keep us from really living our lives and living them in the present.

In fact, some of these distractions corrupt our minds and push us in exactly the wrong directions. Social media time can be spent dwelling upon the past. We look at pictures of ex-girlfriends or ex-boyfriends. We look up old friends and stalk them instead of reaching out and reconnecting. We look at profiles of our more successful acquaintances and wish we'd made their life choices. All of this keeps us from actually making positive changes in our present, or even thinking much about our present.

Then, we turn on the TV and watch shows where we dream about someday having the lives of the people on screen. Someday, we'll have that big house or that perfect job or that ideal romantic partner. Someday, we'll travel like these show hosts. We dream these dreams and leave it at that. There's no time to actually make a change, we've distracted away all the hours of our day.

In such a distracted age, we have to be particularly conscious of our every moment. At this point, we are at peace with our past. Our next goal is to get used to using every moment of our present. While we all know we only have a limited amount of time on this earth, these distractions try to make us forget the clock is running. If we want to discover our 12 Streams of Income and Fulfillment, we've got to start moving, and start moving now.

Like I said, this isn't easy. To get you moving on the right path, you need these seven steps. Each one of these steps is designed to focus your mind on this moment, so that you make sure every step you take is moving you in the right direction and at the right speed, so that, before you know it, you're standing right there on the banks of your 12 Streams.

With the door open, you've got the fresh breeze of opportunity blowing upon your cheek. You've come a long way already, and you should be proud of yourself. But now is not the time to take a break. Now's the time to step down from the porch and walk out into the world to seize your success.

Write down some of the biggest distractions that keep you living in the past and future. How can you limit your time with those distractions and limit their influence?

_____

_____

_____

_____

_____

_____

_____

_____

CHAPTER 10

Getting Used to Living in the Present

As I mentioned in the last chapter, most of us are simply not used to living in the present. We spend our time daydreaming forward or analyzing backward. Instead of taking on the tasks in front of us, we end up delaying what is immediate so we can concentrate on what is gone or what may never be.

This is natural to some extent, but your success doesn't exist in either the past or the future. It exists in the now.

To firmly place your focus on this moment, while still utilizing all the lessons you've taken from the past, you'll need to get used to committing your attention to right now. That's what our first four steps out the door are meant to do for us. With each of these steps, you are getting a little closer to attaining all that you are destined for.

You can think about this like David taking the steps required to reach his kingship. David, above all others, knew how to view his world clearly (as we will, too, in Step 1). He had to, if he wanted to survive. He also allowed himself to be open and influenced by those who were wiser (Step 2). Throughout his life, he listened to Samuel, Nathan, and other wise men. To protect himself and further his goals, he took on new allies wherever he could (Step 3). At first, he came to Saul, and when Saul abandoned him, he found new friends. Above all, despite the many mistakes he made, David always trusted God above all else (Step 4).

In other words, David, as we already knew, went through all this, just on a far more dramatic stage. He can show us the way forward. With these four steps, we start on the same path as David toward our own kingship or queenship. Like David, we're going to learn to snatch every moment and make the most of it.

In order to discover our 12 Streams of Income and Fulfillment, we have to channel our inner David and step boldly out onto the battlefield that is our present. We have to march step-by-step out our door and away from the safety of the home we've built in our past.

That strength and wisdom is still there for us, the security of that home is still behind us, but we need to turn away from that building and look forward, so we can transition from glancing at our potential to living it.

Step 1: Clear Your Vision to Focus on the Moment

Your first step is really just a matter of resetting the way you view your life. This is less active than it is mental. You've become used to looking at the world a certain way, and that will make you resistant to making new progress now that we're beyond coming to terms with your past and becoming active in your present.

Even some of what you've learned already in this book has to be reframed. Before this moment, in this book, we've gone through your experiences, one by one, and tried to refocus them into the positive, strength-building events that they were.

What you have to do now is simultaneously take those positive lessons from those events and try to leave behind all the negative things that have developed out of living through those moments.

What do I mean by that? I mean it's time to shed all that is clouding your vision.

Think about cataracts. A cataract is a clouding of the lens of your eye that develops because of time, wear and tear, and genetics. It comes upon you slowly, so you may not notice it at first. Then, when you do notice, you might make slight corrections to deal with the issue, like reading under brighter light or getting a stronger glass's prescription. Over time, though, if left untreated, that cataract is going to make your vision worse and worse, until you can barely see out of that eye. Through no real fault of your own (other than, perhaps, a choice not to get treated), you can become blind to all that is around you.

So, too, your collective experiences can slowly and subtly cloud your vision of your present moment. You've brought with you through experience, time, and perhaps some genetics, certain biases, certain skepticisms, certain prejudices, and certain pessimisms. In your day-to-day life, you don't notice these things because you've already adjusted your life to compensate for these issues.

Perhaps you have issues trusting authority figures, so you've configured your life so that you hardly ever come into contact with anyone with any significant authority. I'm not saying you were wrong to do this. I'm not saying there wasn't a good reason to behave that way, or you were unwise at some point to do that. I'm saying, to move forward, you're going to have to come to terms with that choice and correct it. Because, as it stands, you may be blinding yourself to the most important opportunities of your life, just because you can't *see* who is offering them to you.

Likewise, you may have decided, long ago, that you are going to live in a particular area. Perhaps that's because your family is there, or it has some deep connection for you. That is absolutely understandable, but if you are so determined to stay in that one place, you are blinding yourself to what may be the fulfillment of your potential that could exist elsewhere. You may be sure you never want to leave your small town or your city on the coast, but what would you do if your dreams could be fulfilled on the other side of the country? Or the other side of the world?

When I was recovering from my low point, I was looking for a new way to make my way in the world. But I was burned out. For a long time, I was blind to any opportunity; I just couldn't stand to see it. When I finally opened my eyes, I saw an unexpected new option in my path: network marketing. That was a job I'd never considered in my life. It wasn't something I knew anything about, and if it had appeared a year earlier, I wouldn't have seen it at all. As it was, when I finally was able to see again, I saw that that may be the job that could lead me to my dreams. And I was right.

Our 12 Streams of Income and Fulfillment can lead us in some very unexpected directions. To reach them, we may have to take some unexpected twists and turns. You have to clear your vision enough to see the way forward.

Thankfully, cataracts can be treated these days. The surgery to fix them is very safe. It's possible to recover your sight and see as clearly as ever. A reason to be even more thankful: clearing your emotional vision doesn't even take surgery. All you have to do is make a conscious effort to identify where old ideas are holding you back and clear those ideas away.

Step 2: Open Yourself to New Influences

Now that we have reoriented ourselves to see what is around us more clearly, we can focus on taking in some of those new influences and possibilities.

As we saw in Step 1, we may always intend to be open, but we can end up unconsciously blinding ourselves from the path we need to follow. Likewise, we can become resistant to receiving new perspectives on how we are living and the choices we are making. These new perspectives can come from anywhere. They may come from our oldest friends and family. They may come from our newest acquaintances. They may come from a movie we just saw, a TV show we love, or a book. In fact, right now, reading this book, you are already engaging in Step 2 because if we are doing anything here, we're exploring new perspectives and considering new influences.

Key 5: Trust the Moment

At this point, you're four keys in. You've learned to trust who you are, what you know, the direction your instinct points you, and the honesty of your speech. You may well be wondering, then, what's left.

This last key is a little different from the others. All the other keys that open the door to your potential are trust issues that exist largely inside you. You have to trust the person you are and know that's the right person for the job ahead. You have to trust that you are knowledgeable, experienced, and wise enough for all the decisions you'll need to take. You have to trust that the direction you've steered your life is the one that will bring you success. And you have to trust that your words have meaning, and when you promise yourself success, you'll achieve it.

All of that trust revolves around your internal feelings and external behavior. Key 5, however, involves not you so much as this moment in time itself.

With that in mind, here's one of the most important pieces of wisdom you'll find in this book: you're right on time, and you're right where you need to be. This is the right moment for your success.

No matter what time it is in your life, whether you're 9 or 90 years old, this is the moment for you. I know that can be hard to accept, but no matter your circumstances or your age, this is the place you're supposed to be. If you'd gotten here a little earlier, you wouldn't have been ready. You wouldn't have had the walls built up around you to provide enough support. If you'd gotten here a little later, it would've been too late. The walls would have begun to crumble because the moment had passed.

I know time can add a funny kind of pressure to the idea of success. We often take a look at the clock when we think about wanting to achieve something. In our dreams, we were all great successes by 20 years of age, and now, we're a little (or a lot) older, and it hasn't come yet. Does that mean it'll never come? Does that mean it's too late?

I'm not saying you should just listen to the ideas of anyone and everyone about you and just follow that advice uncritically, but you need to be receptive. You have to be receptive because, when we're seeing clearly, we know that what we've been doing so far hasn't been working.

Throughout my life, I've needed to explore new perspectives to find a way to move closer to my 12 Streams. At first, I needed new influences to move beyond the violent and dangerous world of the inner city. Then, I needed new influences to find a way to get back up after my real estate business failed. I've needed to find new influences to complete this book. You could say that my life would never have gotten anywhere if I hadn't been willing to take in the influence of God and the godly...but we'll get to that more in Step 4.

These new influences can help you reshape how you pursue your goals. They can also help you discover and reshape what your goals are in the first place.

Success never looks quite like what we think it does when we imagine it. When I was a child, I thought success looked like a fancy car and being able to do whatever I wanted. I didn't know that success would look like a nice real estate office, a good home, the love and safety of my children, and the chance to share this vision with you. I know some people who always thought success was getting into the NBA or selling out big stadiums to perform their music. Others saw success as living like Anthony Bourdain, traveling the world full-time, doing...something. Or maybe nothing.

All of those stories of success do become real success stories for some people, but they aren't necessary your success story. If you are over 18 years, and you didn't make it onto a good NCAA team, and the NBA hasn't called to see if you want to participate in the draft, it isn't going to happen. That isn't your success story. That doesn't mean your life is a failure; it means you need a new perspective on how to look at success and to look for success.

You have to be open to new ideas, new ways of achieving what you want to achieve, and new approaches to your old difficulties.

If someone had told me when I was young that part of what success would mean to me would be writing a book, I would have laughed them right out of the room. Me? Write a book? I didn't even like reading back then. But I found a way to open myself up, and in opening, I found that this was an important part of my journey.

Remember, you aren't looking for just one stream, one way to make your fortune and give your life meaning. There are twelve. To reach all of them, you have to accept new ideas and possibilities throughout your journey.

With so many streams, there's plenty of room for creative new ways to approach and achieve things. So many, in fact, I can't even begin to name them here. I can't tell you the paths that will work for you or the streams you will find at the end. What I can tell you is that the world is going to show you those things. So, keep an open mind when you see new ideas.

Step 3: Look for Allies

Even the most dedicated, brilliant person in the world is going to have to work with others to achieve their goals. Steve Jobs couldn't build the iPhone on his own. He may have been the brilliant mind behind it, but he wouldn't have gotten very far with his ideas without a huge number of designers, programmers, managers, marketers, and many others.

Like Jobs, you'll need allies to discover your 12 Streams of Income and Fulfillment. To achieve anything of significance, you will have to look for people you can work with or work for. You'll need to look for people who can give you a hand getting started or getting your name out there.

No one climbs the ladder to success on their own. We all need some allies. Who will your allies be? I can't tell you. They may be the same people you've relied on your whole life. It may be parents and siblings, or your best friend since age five who gives you that much needed boost. It may also be someone who you haven't even met yet. It could be a colleague you meet next year who is willing to take the time outside work to help you build up the brand identity you need to launch your own company. It may be an acquaintance or a shared friend who gives you the vital gift of believing in your dreams when you finally share them.

In all likelihood, it will be some combination of all the people in your life that help you along. The help they will give you will be of many different sorts. Some of it may be spiritual, some of it may be emotional, some of it may be physical (helping you move things into your new shop, for instance), and some of it may be financial. But they will all touch your life and uplift you. You just have to be open to taking on all the allies you need to get where you're going.

My own journey has involved a lot of allies. They started with my grand-mother, who taught me the most important lessons of my life and always believed in me. But while she was my greatest ally, she wasn't the only one who got me where I am today. I also needed my kids and my wife to support me, love me, and believe in me. I needed my pastor to inspire me and connect me to the power of God. I needed friends, and I needed business partners. They say it takes a village to raise a child, but in my experience, it also takes a village to raise a man or woman up to success.

Taking your journey to success into the present and accepting the help you need to make progress can be awkward, embarrassing, and uncom-fortable. For all that, we have to do it, because we never know who will be the fateful person who gives us that major hand up, the one that makes all the difference.

Step 4: Look to God

I end this chapter on this step, and I place it right in the middle of all the steps because in some ways, it is the most central point. Through this step, all others flow.

Every person who believes in God knows one, true fact about life: Nothing is possible without God. I wouldn't be here without God, and I wouldn't be anything without God. My life, my joy, and my success I all owe to God.

This goes beyond just a deep sense of faith, though. God has been more than a distant, spiritual concept to me. He has played an active role in my life. After all, it was through His revelation that I came to understand the 12 Streams of Income and Fulfillment. It was through my faith that I was able to recover from my lowest moments and find the strength to try again.

Moreover, it was through my fellow believers that I found wisdom and light in the darkness. It was my pastor, Bishop David Evans, who helped me through many of my most difficult moments. It was the power of his faith in God and his faith in me that allowed me to recover from every blow.

For those of us who believe, we know that God is an active element in life. He is present in our choices, in our joys and sorrows, and in our community. It would be inconceivable to take a single step without God, and almost blasphemous to consider taking such a huge journey in life without putting Him first in all our thoughts and actions.

God makes it possible for us to achieve these grand dreams. As Paul told the Philippians, "I can do all this through Him who gives me strength."

God is more than strength, though. God is also the key to remaining focused in this moment and viewing your coming success with the right perspective. For all the inspiration God provides you, He also demands from you a focus beyond yourself. It is only through God that you can remain grounded, humble, and grateful. As we head toward streams that provide not just income but also fulfillment, that godly perspective is key to making that success feel fulfilled.

I know not all of you reading this believe in God. For those of you who do not, I urge you to still find that spiritual center that brings you strength. Find those who share your beliefs, whatever they are, and use that connection to lift each other up. While there is no replacement for God, there is a place in all our hearts that requires meaning, faith, and purpose. Fill that, or else, you'll never be able to count anything a success in life.

Plot a path forward in your everyday life that incorporates the first four steps. How can you remove the cataracts that block your vision? How can you open yourself to new influences and allies? How can you bring God and spirituality into a more central position in your life?

_____

_____

_____

_____

_____

_____

_____

_____

_____

_____

CHAPTER 11

Avoiding Those Trips and Falls

We are now comfortably in our stride, making progress toward our 12 Streams of Income and Fulfillment. We are close enough to hear the streams flowing, to feel the wet spray of the water on the breeze, and to almost reach out and take a sip from those meaning-giving streams.

However, being so close can breed a certain kind of overconfidence. We may start running and forget to watch our step. At that point, we can easily trip, fall, and end up broken, so close to the long-awaited moment.

As with the previous four steps, we have seen this all before with David. David was blindsided by unexpected setbacks and betrayals (Step 5). He had to be able to adapt his strategies and expectations whenever the situation in front of him changed (Step 6). And he had to have the wisdom to remain focused on what was most important and what his true goals were (Step 7). It was only through his deft handling of these steps that David was able to ever get his career off the ground, and ever become the man and king we still admire, thousands of years later.

For you, too, this is a moment to be particularly careful. We need to prepare for anything that might cause us harm or delay us on our journey. These last three steps are the most precarious, but when we follow them carefully and combine them with the four we've already covered, we can reach our streams in record time.

Step 5: Expect Surprises

We've just discussed in the last chapter how nothing ever comes together quite as we imagine it. Success probably won't look exactly like what we thought it would, whether we first imagined it as a child or at age sixty. To discover our streams, we'll need the help of unexpected individuals in unexpected circumstances, guided by unexpected influences. In the same way, there are going to be surprises along the way in your everyday present. You plan to launch a website, and you discover there's a problem with the design that requires a significant delay. You plan to apply for a great job, but personal difficulties make it impossible, and you see that opportunity pass you by. You want to propose and start your family, but financial limitations mean you have to put it off.

Putting a popular old phrase more politely, "stuff happens." And that's okay. If discovering your 12 Streams was easy, you wouldn't need a book. You'd already have all you ever wanted.

It's okay for things to go a little off track. You simply have to be able to adapt to the surprises that creep up on you. Put another way: The best plans don't come off without a hitch; you have to *plan* for the hitches.

Even a relatively smooth path to your streams will have some obstacles. There will be stones and boulders, roots and debris, which can trip you up. There are few successful lives in history that enjoyed a straight path without obstacles. Before Steve Jobs became "the man who invented the iPhone," he was kicked out of his own company. He spent years in exile from Apple, considered by many a failure, before being recalled to his old position and given his chance to discover his full potential.

Similarly, the life of Abraham Lincoln is full of electoral losses and business struggles, right up until he ran for president in 1860. That didn't stop him from becoming perhaps the greatest president in our country's history. Look a little beyond the narrative of success attached to most of the great men and women we admire, and you'll find a lot of unhappy surprises in their lives that they had to overcome.

Your life and my life are no different than Jobs', Lincoln's, or David's lives. We will have surprises that hit us even this close to our success. The point is to learn from the examples of these greats, anticipate the unexpected setback, and raise your level of determination to overcome whatever hits you, whenever it hits you.

This is a step I struggled with a great deal. After my real estate business collapsed, I struggled to see how a setback is different than a complete failure. It took me years to understand that I had actually just stumbled on the way to my streams, but I hadn't fallen. I was still on the path. In fact, I needed that difficulty to make sure I was going right where I needed to be.

If you find yourself tripping up just before you discover your streams, commit yourself now to getting up, brushing yourself off, and getting going again, right away. Skinned knees, black eyes, bruised elbows: it doesn't matter. You're going to discover your success, no matter what is in your way.

Step 6: Exercise Your Flexibility

When you come across those surprises, to overcome them, you're going to have to challenge yourself to be flexible. If you've ever forgotten to stretch before a run, you know that you feel the strain more. And, if you encounter an obstacle in your path, you'll struggle more to leap over it or navigate around it. You just aren't limber enough to handle it. Your body isn't flexible enough to keep your stride and get beyond what is in your way.

It's the same way with the surprises that will make trouble for you going forward. They don't have to cause you much harm or delay, but they will test your ability to find a flexible solution without losing momentum.

Take the examples we considered in the last step. If there are problems with your website that delay your launch, you'll have to find flexible solutions. Someone who isn't being flexible may try to break their piggy bank and pay someone to fix it in hours instead of days. That would mean they'd take on huge risk if they couldn't recover that money quickly through their new site. A more flexible person might turn this same situation into an advantage. They might use it to redesign those pages of the site they weren't too fond of before. They might shift work over to the Facebook page for a few days while the issues are fixed. They might offer discounts to customers who found the situation inconvenient, which might inspire them to come back more often.

A bit of flexibility could turn a major fall into a small bump in the road, and one that didn't really affect the road to success.

Likewise, missing out on a job can be very upsetting and frustrating, but it can represent—to a flexible person—an opportunity to sharpen skills or expand the search for the right job further. That perfect job set in a town you don't like may give way to a job in the city of your dreams if you are willing to take the surprise in stride. You may also find, in being flexible and brave enough to inquire into the post, that other jobs are on the horizon with that same company. Or new connections might be made that open up a new path to you.

Finally, having to put off a much-dreamed-of wedding can feel almost soul crushing when you want to make that life-long promise to the love of your life, but that year spent saving may add the extra strength and grounding your relationship needs to survive all the other surprises ahead in life. It may be in that year that you finally see other aspects of your dreams begin to flourish. And, you'll know the person you are with is willing to love you, wait for you, and stand by you, even when money is tight.

In all of the above situations, a little flexibility transforms the struggle into a positive experience. This should all seem pretty familiar, since this is precisely what we've been doing with our old difficulties in life. All that time spent within the house on the hill was limbering you up so you can be flexible now.

Step 7: Keep Sight of Your Goals, Even as They Shift

The first and the last steps of this process are really about focus, and that similarity is intentional. While the first step is about refocusing yourself to get beyond your past and to see and live in the present clearly, this last step is about keeping your eyes on the prize, even when that prize is a moving target.

This is different from fixating on a dream future. I'm not telling you to sit around and just think about how much you want to live in a mansion. What I'm saying is that you need to avoid focusing so much on the moment-to-moment that you forget where you're going. There's a difference between standing around and looking at the scenery and watching where you're going when you're moving quickly. We want nothing to do with the former, but the latter is incredibly important.

In other words, you need to keep your eyes on your feet as you move step-by-step because you don't want to trip and fall. But that doesn't mean you can take your eyes off the streams ahead. You've got to look at both your feet and where you're going all at once. This can be crucial because your streams may not remain stationary. Sometimes, they move.

Let's consider an example. Let's say you have always wanted to be a doctor. You decide you're going to take out the loans and go back to school. You overcome the difficulties of your past, use your new wisdom, and follow step-by-step toward that goal.

However, as you take classes, you discover you don't actually like medicine. What you like is the idea of helping people, but medicine itself doesn't feel like the right way to do that anymore. Instead, you discover that what you are really good at is talking to people who are struggling with something.

Someone focused only on taking each step might brush aside this feeling. You can become mesmerized by the act of taking your steps and obsessed with meeting a single, specific goal. This stubborn refusal to look up can mean you don't give yourself a chance to make sure you're still going the right way.

Someone who doesn't look up may end up spending hundreds of thousands of dollars to achieve a dream they didn't actually want. They'd discover a stream, and find the income in it, but not the fulfillment. It wasn't their stream after all.

Looking up, though, before getting so far down the path, they could find their stream is actually just off to the side. It's actually social work that they always wanted to do. Before they took a class, they didn't have that idea quite in their head. They didn't have a name for it. Looking up after making some progress, though, they could see it clearly.

There's that clear sight again. There's the need for flexibility. There's the surprise that came out of nowhere.

That's why we have the idea of vision placed at the beginning and the end of these steps. You need to always be seeing clearly all that is around you. You can't take a single step if you're approaching it blindly. You have to see your past clearly, your surroundings clearly, the obstacles in front of you clearly, and your goals clearly.

When you see everything as clearly and unbiasedly as possible, you know you are following your true heart and your true path. Having that clarity allows you to rejuvenate your dedication to the process, even in the tough moments. You can look yourself in the mirror and say, "I know where I've been, I know where I'm going, and I know it's all good."

And you'll know, when you say it, that you mean it, every syllable. When you are going the right way and doing it all the right way, you can know—one hundred percent—you're going to get there.

Plot a path forward in your everyday life that incorporates the last three steps. How can you better prepare for surprises? How can you become more flexible in unexpected moments? How can you keep sight of your goals while also keeping sight of what you're doing in the moment?

_____

_____

_____

_____

_____

_____

_____

_____

_____

_____

_____

_____

CHAPTER 12

All Steps, All the Time

As we come now to the banks of your 12 Streams of Income and Fulfillment, it is important to recognize something about all of these steps: they don't necessarily happen in order. In fact, these aren't really seven individual steps you will take one at a time. They are part of every step you take from here until you discover your streams.

Just as the 12 Walls of Support before might not have occurred in the order described, and all 5 Keys of Trust occur all at once and all the time in practice, so too the 7 Steps to Your Potential should be with you and active at all times.

The real trick in preparing for your 12 Streams is in incorporating all of this wisdom into your everyday life. You have to strive to use the strength and wisdom from your vast and sometimes troublesome experience, engage in all forms of trust, and develop the right kinds of focus and tactics to navigate the present, and you have to do it all the time.

This can seem overwhelming, but simply by being conscious of these factors, you are already engaging in them more. Like a muscle, the more you work these factors out in your life, the more they will grow stronger until it is second nature to employ all of them, all at once, all the time.

I'm not saying this is always easy, or that there won't be moments when you slip up, but you now have the map that leads to the accomplishments you were always destined for.

Often, the difficulty in creating success in life is not in finding the energy, will, or desire to be successful; it's in not knowing how to achieve it. In that sense, you are now already far closer to your 12 Streams, even if you've just been lying in bed, reading this book in a single night. If you've spent years, perhaps most of your life, in that dark corner in a room, without even a passing glance at the life you want to be living, you now know how to get up, get out, and get to the place you've only ever dreamed of.

This map came to me in pieces, inspired by divine inspiration. Even with all this insight, I, too, have stumbled, fallen, gotten lost, and gone off track at times. We're all fallible, imperfect, and no matter how clearly we try to see, we will all make mistakes.

I'm not telling you this to discourage you. I'm telling you this so you know that wherever you are on this path today, wherever you are tomorrow, and wherever you are next year, you're making progress and you're heading in the right direction. Now that you know the direction to head and how to head there, I can tell you that you're going to get to those 12 Streams.

This is a divinely sanctioned path. We have seen already in this book that many of the most successful and inspiring people in the modern world have taken this path. We've also seen how David and others in the Bible have done the same. They've all made mistakes in their past; they've all dealt with real difficulties. They've all had to engage in extreme levels of trust. They've all had to find a way to live and make progress in the present instead of dwelling on the past or the future.

They've shown us the way forward. God has made the process clear. All that is left now is to commit to this effort so that we can all discover our 12 Streams of Income and Fulfillment.

Turning Toward the Banks of Our 12 Streams

But what are those 12 Streams? Now that we stand upon the banks of those streams, with so much work and experience behind us, we're finally close enough to see precisely what each of these streams really are and what they mean. We've finally reached the moment where we can clearly define all the individual ways that we can make the money we deserve, live our ideal lives, and do the work that will provide us with a sense of purpose.

Before we dive into those streams, though, I want you to take a moment to look backward. For just for a moment, look back at all the way you've come from that dark corner. Think about the walls you've seen and navigated around, the keys you've found and used to open the door to your potential, the steps you've taken down the steep hill to these very streams. The way wasn't always easy, but you have proven already that you have what it takes within you to overcome all obstacles to reach this point. So, take this moment, take a long glance, feel grateful, and feel proud.

Now, turn around, face forward, turn the page, and meet your 12 Streams of Income and Fulfillment.

SECTION IV.

THE 12 STREAMS
OF INCOME
AND FULFILLMENT

CHAPTER 13

Orienting Yourself to Your Streams

At long last, after a long spiritual journey through all your lived experience, you have discovered the flowing streams that represent the true and perfect means of achieving all the income and fulfillment you are destined to achieve.

You've traveled a great distance to get here—from that corner of the room, to the doorway, down the hill, and into this valley. But we've spent enough time there already. The streams are flowing right underfoot. It's time to jump in and swim in your potential.

Instead of focusing on the past, let's take a look at what is around us now. Trace the path of the streams on every side of you. These 12 streams belong only to you. Your streams are different from mine and from everyone else's. Where they came from, where they're going, and what opportunities float within exist solely for you. Without realizing it, you've been carving out the path these streams would flow from the day you were born.

That kind of individual, singular, destined success can feel intimidating. Now that you're outside, exposed to the world, there are no corners to hide in anymore. You're out in the open and receiving the reward you've worked so hard for all comes down to you now. There's no room for excuses. I'm going to show you the streams; it's up to you to use them.

This moment is for you, but it's also on you. So, make the most of that by realizing what is in front of you and how to make the most of it.

The Source of the Streams

To understand your 12 Streams of Income and Fulfillment, I need you to understand where they've come from. I've just said you created them, and that's true, but the ability to create these streams comes from a far higher power with a far higher purpose. This is the heart of the revelation I received from God. When I opened my Bible on that fateful night, I was guided to two particular passages: 1 Samuel 16 and Revelations 21. It was through the revelations in these two passages that it became clear to me how we could all construct twelve streams for ourselves.

In many ways, these two passages couldn't be further apart. One has to do with Israel's greatest king, David, the man who has already framed much of our vision of success in this book. The other has to do with the end of times, the Second Coming, and ultimate salvation.

David is far into the past. He's ancient history. Revelations describes our collective future, near or far. And yet, as with so much of the Bible, there are unseen threads that connect these passages together. Once you see what these passages are saying beneath the surface, you can start to see how God is guiding each and every one of us to the income and the fulfillment of purpose He has always had planned for us.

So, before we visit our streams individually, let's take a moment to explore what those two passages say on the surface and how they connect below that.

1 Samuel 16 is a particularly famous passage. It's famous because that is where we first meet David. The David we meet isn't yet a fierce warrior-king, the conqueror of lands, the victor over Saul, or the great poet of the Psalms. We don't meet David in his glory. Instead, we meet a humble, simple David

who is no more than just another shepherd…at least on the surface. However, within this passage are the seeds of what will make David great, and what also makes each of us great. In a single chapter, we see how David has four areas in which his excellence could show through. If he follows through on all of those four areas, he will be Israel's greatest king. If not, he will remain a simple shepherd. It's all in his hands. God has set the path forward; David has to take it.

Keep those four areas in mind because that brings us to Revelations 21. In this chapter, we learn about the New Jerusalem. The Lord assures John, the author of the book, "Behold, I make all things new," and "Write, for these words are true and faithful."

John then goes on to describe the city of New Jerusalem, the glorious deliverance of God's promise at the end of times. This city has a high wall with twelve gates: "Three gates on the east, three gates on the north, three gates on the south, and three gates on the west."

John then sees twelve foundations to this city, each made from a precious material.

Like I said, on first inspection, it seems that these two passages couldn't be more different. And yet, there are four holy categories in both. In 1 Samuel, we see the four seeds of David's glory in his early life. In Revelations, we see the glory of God flowing in four directions. When we combine these ideas together, we can see the four cardinal directions pointing toward the four ways we can create success in life. And in each direction, there are three "gates," or in our case, "streams" that spread out this success, allowing all those precious metals and jewels to flow into our own lives.

In other words, if we discover the four elements God has planted within each of us, and expand those four elements in three ways, we open ourselves to the wealth and fulfillment we were always destined to find.

Why three, though? Why don't we look for four or five ways to maximize these areas? The reason is simple. It isn't just that God has commanded it this way. He's commanded it this way because three is so achievable. Coming up with three ways to expand one main stream takes a few minutes. More streams, and there wouldn't be time to tend to all of them. Three streams in each direction and you can easily focus on each one when you need to.

God's plan for us is to use all that He has given us to achieve untold good and receive untold wealth as a means to bring His glory to Earth. The meaning couldn't be clearer.

You may ask why I didn't reveal this upfront in this book, but the answer is within the pages you've already read as well as in the Bible itself. David may have had all these elements within himself from birth, but he had a long journey to go on before he could collect the wisdom necessary to pursue his success. Likewise, John didn't immediately see the city of New Jerusalem. He, too, had a journey first before he was worthy of the vision he received. We must all go on the journey God has planned for us. Only then, once we have collected the skills and knowledge we need, can we take this revelation and transform it into our individual success.

You had to go through your struggle. You had to make those mistakes in your past. You had to get knocked down and get back up and get knocked down again. Only by living that struggle and understand that struggle could you possibly be in a position to use all 12 of your Streams of Income and Fulfillment.

Now, we've got those skills and the knowledge. We've got the motivation and intention. We understand where we've been and where we are. All we need is to take the Word of God as our guide and dive into our streams. There's no need for further delay. Let's begin sketching out the pathway to our income and fulfillment.

CHAPTER 14

Your Streams to the East: Your Job

W e begin in the east, where the sun rises and hope always arrives, and where our first streams are set. While that sunrise is a romantic sign of the new dawn of our life, this first set of streams is in some ways the least romantic. These streams are also the ones that continue over most from the life you've been living. That's because in the east, we find the source of income that is the most "traditional": your job.

Face it: you may not like your job, you may not want to go to it, but you're probably good at it. If you've been working in an office for fifteen years, you know what you're doing, and you know how to do it. I know a lot of books like this will draw you in with promises that you can just quit your job and live a romantic life on an island with almost no effort. You can just do A, B, and C, and you can say goodbye to the uninspiring but stable job you've had for years.

That may be possible in the rarest of circumstances, but it isn't really how life works, and I'm not going to lie to you and pretend it is. Your job is an important part of your life. It's part of who you are, and it's crucial you have that money coming so you can expand your income and fulfillment potential elsewhere.

Don't despair. After all, again, this is something you're good at. Your 9–5—whether you're a laborer, a police officer, a waiter, or an accountant—is something you are an expert at. That's why you've fallen into this job and why you've kept it so long. When you look at it that way, as a part of your life where you are already a kind of success, your job can seem far more appealing.

But why do we hate our day job so much? Often, it's not the occupation itself; it's the particulars of the job and the lack of outside fulfillment. What I mean is you may be the best secretary in your office, and you may constantly get more work without ever getting a raise. That is a recipe for disillusionment. Your boss doesn't appreciate you. They don't pay you what you're worth. And you don't have anything else in your life to give you any hope or joy. However, that doesn't mean you should quit being a secretary and make reckless life changes. You're good at being a secretary. That just means you should be a secretary somewhere else. By all means, check the ads and look for a better place of employment, but don't give up what you're good at just because the trappings of the job aren't what they should be.

At the same time, we often dislike our job because it becomes so central to everything in our lives. It's our sole source of income. It's our sole source of activity outside the house. It's our sole focus and sole source of self-worth. When all you have is your job as a secretary, it's easy to dwell upon all the little injustices and difficulties that come with the job. We can come to resent anything when we put it in that position. Even if you had your dream job, if that's all you had, you would come to feel all those same negative feelings over time. Anytime our job lets us down, we feel it throughout our lives, and we end up hating our job for the power it has over us.

And then, combining those two elements, there's an issue with feeling like your job is holding you back. Life is difficult when you feel stuck. You sense, quite rightly, that you are capable of more than being a secretary, and you start to feel it's the job as a secretary that is the problem. When you're working and things just aren't happening for you, you can begin to feel like you don't enjoy that work anymore. It may have been a job you were once excited about, but now that it hasn't delivered on all its promise, you begin to hate even the parts you once found most enjoyable.

You used to enjoy talking to your colleagues. You used to enjoy fielding calls and organizing the office's day. Now, because things aren't moving forward elsewhere in life, you resent those things you used to enjoy.

It's the same in any job. You may have been a teacher for thirty years. In that time, you've gone from an idealist who loves the work to someone who is sick of the routine. You know the material; you know the expectations; and now all you do is prepare kids for tests. The passion and creativity have been sapped out. You can do the job with your eyes closed. Now, you just see the paychecks that don't get any bigger, the extra outside-the-class work, and the lack of recognition. Sometimes, that makes you want to move on. Sure, the job is paying the bills. But that's *all* it is doing. Sure, you're good at it, but you want something different.

I know what I'm talking about here. My wife's a teacher, and she's amazing at it. Yet, she also has times when she gets burned out and just doesn't want to ever see a classroom again. My middle daughter works in a hospital. She's good at it. But all the stress of the job can get her down sometimes. When it's been a while without a vacation and the paychecks aren't growing and the career isn't advancing, it can be hard to get up and get back to a job like that.

Look, I'm not trying to devalue your distaste for your job. I know that many people reading this book are doing so precisely because they are dissatisfied with their current job. What I am trying to say is that your job is an absolutely central part of your present and future success. You may not like your job, and that's okay. However, if you are good at what you do, you should do it. I'll go further than that—you *must* do it. That doesn't mean you have to stay in the office you're in, or at the school you're teaching at, or at the restaurant you're serving at, but you should stick with what you're good at.

You just shouldn't let it take over your life any longer. Quite the opposite, in fact. You should let your job fall further back in your mental priorities. This is only one of the directions for your income and fulfillment. Seeing it as one part of four can help you realize that you are not your job, and your work doesn't have to influence everything else in your life.

Many people work in a job with the sole goal of getting out. They want to get out because they invest their job with negativity, and because their job is so important, that negativity overtakes everything. However, when the other parts of your life are working, then that one area of your life doesn't have such a stronghold of negativity.

David's Job

If you aren't sure your job is good enough to be your job, just consider how David made his money early in life. In 1 Sam 16:11, we discover that David's job was perhaps the least glorified in all of ancient Israel. He was required to "keepeth the sheep" for his family. He was a shepherd.

I don't know how much thought you've ever put into what it means to be a shepherd, but it wasn't a very nice job. Sheep stink. They're hard to watch because they love to wander off. The job is also a boring one. You'd spend days on a hill just watching animals eat grass. There's no one to talk to. There's very little to do to entertain yourself. If you fall asleep, you might lose a sheep, and so lose a lot of money, since sheep are your whole business.

The job is stinky, hard, and boring. On top of all that, it could be dangerous. There were dangerous animals in the wilderness, and David had to be prepared to fight for his life all the time, just protect his stinky investment. How bad is your job in comparison to that?

David's job was bad enough, many of us would have wanted to quit on Day 1. But sheep were good business in the ancient world. Wool was responsible for much of the clothing, and so sheep were a sure thing. They produced. David didn't necessarily like those stinking, hard hearing, stubborn wandering sheep. He certainly didn't like risking his life getting his sheep back from lions and bears. But it paid the bills, so he stuck with it.

My Streams in the East

My job in real estate isn't nearly as bad as being a shepherd, I know, but I, too, have had my share of negative feelings in this area. I know the real estate business. I've made a lot of money in real estate. Real estate has fed, clothed, and sheltered my family. I'm grateful for it. For all that, though, I don't always like the work. That doesn't mean I'll ever walk away from it, though. It's what I'm good at. It's my job. It's a central stream in my income and fulfillment. I don't want to leave my job. I want to maximize the income I get from this job.

This is where the beauty of the streams comes in because they teach us how to get more not just from what we want but from what we already have. If I told you my job was "real estate," you might think that counts as the whole of my eastern streams. Just sell a house and make some money. In fact, there are *three* streams here to account for:

1. Working with buyers and sellers

2. Investing in renovating local real estate

3. Developing a mortgage company

All of the sudden, my income isn't just based on one aspect of the real estate world. I've expanded my potential into multiple areas. Now, I'm protected against shortfalls in one area and able to expand in other areas. This flexibility frees me from some of those crushing concerns and some of the daily drudgery that make a job seem like a struggle instead of a blessing. I can work more on one stream on Monday and more on another stream on Tuesday. If one stream runs dry for a season, another stream will flow forth almost to flooding.

Modeling Your Streams in the East

That's not just true of real estate. If you are a teacher, like my wife, you can expand your streams to include private lessons, online classes, or summer school classes. Take a summer and go teach English as a Second Language abroad. Or, look into teaching classes at a local community college. Suddenly, teaching can be exciting again, more lucrative, and with far more opportunities for advancement. Now, "teaching" isn't a single job that takes up all your time, focus, and energy. Instead, your streams look like this:

1. Teaching 8th grade science

2. Teaching ESL over the summer in Italy

3. Giving private lessons in English literature (your true passion) after school

The streams are there, if you go looking for them.

If you're a secretary, you can hire yourself out to startup businesses. You can type up transcripts after hours. You can teach classes on office management or typing. Take a look at online, remote opportunities in this area, and you'll be surprised how many options you actually have, even if you have a set 9-5 schedule Monday through Friday. Even with that schedule your streams are now:

1. Office secretary M-F 9-5

2. Giving typing lessons at local community college

3. Assisting at a local startup you're passionate about

Again, the streams are there, if you go looking for them.

My point here is, your job is not your enemy. It's just you haven't had the opportunity to put it in its proper place in your life. You haven't let the complete its potential flower and open up more income for your life. Once you have all the streams, you'll see that this can be a joyful part of your day, week, and year.

Look, I know you may want to hear something different here. You want to hear that you should just leave the job you're good at because you can just snap your fingers and be something you *think* is more interesting.

I've tried that. Despite being good at real estate, I have walked away from it before. For many years, I did lots of other things. Some of them I liked, some I liked less, but none of those things ever produced for me like real estate did. When I finally came back to real estate, guess what? It started producing all over again. It isn't always what I liked, but I could always do it. That was my sheep. It produced my wool.

I've never woken up in the morning saying, "Oh boy, I'm glad to go out and work in real estate." However, I've learned to be content in it because it produces. More than that, I've learned to find joy in that work and beyond it, thanks to the streams.

David was out there with the sheep instead of at home, despite being the youngest in his family, because he was good at it. He was producing. He could keep those sheep in line by himself, despite being so young. And that job opened up so many opportunities for him. Learning to control those sheep would lead him to many of his other streams, where he would find more fulfilment and a wealth of riches.

Your job is the same. You may not see how being a secretary can lead to wealth and true fulfillment, but these streams are preparing you for success in other areas of your life. You are learning the skills you need to be a success elsewhere as well. The trick isn't quitting and jumping into the unknown. It's expanding. First, expand the streams of your job. Then, move on to the streams of your passion.

Fill in your three streams of the East.

1.

2.

3.

CHAPTER 15

Your Streams to the North: Your Passion

Your three Streams to the East can sometimes feel like a disappointment. After all, you probably entered into this journey not to reinforce the need for that work but to find something new, to find a way to your passion.

The great news is that when you turn your attention to the north, that is precisely what you'll find. While utilizing all 12 Streams of Income and Fulfillment requires you to keep up with the work you are good at naturally, it also leaves plenty of room for you to pursue your passions.

David's Passion

Often, you'll find that your eastern streams lead directly or indirectly into your northern passion streams. Consider David. When he was out in the fields, being a shepherd, he would amuse himself by playing music. That led to him becoming, in 1 Samuel 16:16, "a cunning player on a harp."

David struck up this passion to make his day job more bearable, and yet, just because it started as an amusing passion, that didn't mean there wasn't a way to make that passion produce in a powerful way. It turned out that David's playing could lead to a huge advancement in his career. That music opened the door for him to work for Saul, which set him on the path to do more than just provide for his family, it led him to the way to become the richest and most powerful man of Israel. David didn't abandon being a shepherd to pursue music in the court. He didn't run away from earning to pursue a dream. He kept up the dream while he worked, and then the opening *presented itself* for him to pursue success through his passion.

Your Streams in the North

Your passion can also become a powerful earning tool in your life, but you have to make conscious effort to see where the opportunity presents itself. My passion presented itself in the midst of my greatest struggles. When I had lost my real estate business, and had few opportunities to advance, I discovered a passion that I didn't know existed. That passion is for network marketing.

Now, I'll be honest with you, when I started network marketing, I found a job that I really loved. For some, network marketing is the ideal *job* for them. It provides all those high-earning eastern streams. It wasn't that way for me. I like everything about network marketing. I like traveling. I like getting people fired up. I like seeing people go from knowing nothing to something to allowing that something to produce for them. I like seeing people get from one place to another and watching it produce for them. I liked the whole process, but it just wasn't producing enough for me.

In that job, I produced some income, but not nearly as much as I did and do in real estate. For some, that would create a real dilemma. Do you take a pay cut to follow your passion or do you give up on your passion to maintain your income?

If you look at your income as something that pours in from a single source, this becomes a troubling problem. If, instead, you look at the *streams* of your income, you can suddenly accommodate both your work and your passion. You can allow your work to carry the weight of your major income, while everything you can earn through your passion is just bonus. It's "some more."

That "some more" can expand, just as with the East, into three streams, challenging you to always be building your passion into new potential income opportunities.

For me, I've taken my passion for network marketing and expanded as follows:

1. Network marketing with other companies

2. Creating my own network marketing business

3. Giving motivational speeches and seminars

Modeling Your Streams in the North

Because network marketing is the "some more" in my life, it makes my life better instead of creating difficult burdens and choices. If your passion becomes something you have to do, it can quickly lose its luster. You start attaching more focus to your income from your passion than your joy from your passion. However, if your passion is just what you like to do, then as a result, you'll look forward to it when you're doing what you must do.

And, because you're looking forward to what you like to do, the job you must do doesn't bother you as much anymore. That's because you aren't demanding your job provide an outlet for the passions within you. Now, you're not looking to get away from it anymore, you're grateful for it. After all, it's now buying you the ability to spend the rest of your time earning with your passion.

Your office job doesn't have to change at all, and it can still open the door for you to play music on the weekends—and earn money doing it. You can look at that office job as sponsoring the passion in your life, all while increasing the income available to you.

All the sudden, after you finish work, you now have three new streams of income flowing to you:

1. Playing at local clubs on the weekend

2. Giving guitar lessons in the evening

3. Sitting in as a studio musician on local bands recording albums

Now, you are playing music regularly and you're earning from it. Whether it's a little or a lot, it doesn't matter because your job is still doing the lifting in that area. That opens up the chance for you to just do what you love doing and enjoying all the extras that come with it. That extra may include a fortune, or it may just pay for a family vacation once in a while, but that doesn't matter. You can just let it produce as it needs to and let it flow when it will.

This is the most valuable lesson of the streams. When you allow each part of your life to produce as it should, instead of as you want it to, you remove the pressure of success, which makes the success come more readily. You aren't losing your passion for music because you have to play every night to make ends meet. You're playing because you love it, and that love will show through and lead to greater success.

By removing the pressure to make your passion the center of your life, by putting it in an appropriate place and reducing the stress upon immediate financial success, you open yourself to all kinds of new possibilities. And each one, when you achieve it, will be an extra blessing.

Fill in your three streams of the North.

1.

_____

2.

_____

3.

_____

CHAPTER 16

Your Streams to the South: Your Gift

Many books concentrate on one of two things: finding the right job to make money or finding a way to live off your passion. For a lot of people, this is a binary choice. You can have one or the other, very rarely can you have both. But beyond that...well, there is no beyond that. There's one job; there's one passion. There's no other way to be fulfilled or to fill out your income.

The power of the revelation I received is that it busts open these false choices and allows complete income and fulfillment to rush into your life. We already know that you don't have to choose between your income and your passion. Lived properly, your life is meant to accommodate both.

And it isn't meant to be limited to just those two things either.

Turning our attention south, we can see, somewhat to our surprise, three more fresh, flowing streams of potential. Looking more closely, we can see them taking shape. These streams don't refer to the job that you're good at. They don't refer to the work you're passionate about. No, these streams are something different entirely. They flow out of your innate gift.

What do I mean by "gift"? This is important because the reason so many miss this set of streams is because they don't understand the difference between the southern streams of their gift and the other streams we've already covered.

In your first streams, you saw the work that you are good at and that makes you the most income. You've learned all the skills required for these streams, and you have the experience and knowledge to do well, particularly if you find ways outside of a traditional single job to make more income. In your second set of streams, you found the work that fills you with passion and joy. Here, these streams channel something you love. It may not be the thing you do best in the world, but it's the thing that makes you happy the most when you're doing it. Ability comes out of the love for that activity.

Your gift, on the other hand, is an innate ability within you. That means you're born with it. You didn't discover it. You didn't find it along the way and just stick to it until you figured it out. This is something that was always there, something that is so much a part of you that you may have never thought to harness it for your and your family's betterment.

David's Gift

Let's take a look at David to get a better idea of this. In 1 Sam. 16:18b, we first here that David is "a mighty valiant man" and "a man of war."

Now, at this point, David's never fought anything but the beasts of the wild on behalf of his sheep. He's never led an army, and yet, when viewed through prophetic sight, it was clear that he had a natural gift for strategy and battle.

This is right at the beginning, in our first introduction to David. Seeing him that way, it's no surprise that he would go on to kill Goliath. It may have surprised everyone else, but David knew he could handle it because he knew this gift was there all along.

We can now see the difference between a passion and a gift. David didn't love war. It wasn't what he wanted to do. He wanted to sit around, play the harp, and write some poetry. This was something he naturally was adept at.

He simply "got it" without needing any training. From the first moment he was tested in this field— by all those wild beasts—he was an expert.

My Streams in the South

Not every gift has to be so dramatic. We can't all be gifted warriors on the battlefield (although, undoubtedly, that is the gift for some of you). For me, my gift is a little humbler, but just as fulfilling. My gift is cooking.

Now, I didn't go to school for cooking. I've never been apprenticed to a Michelin-starred restaurant chef. I've never even taken a cooking class, and I've hardly ever read a cookbook. In short, I've had no training in the culinary arts at all.

For all that, though, I know without a doubt that I could have been a chef if I'd ever tried to pursue it. I can go out to dinner, eat the meal, and come home and recreate the same flavor for guests at my house. I don't have to ask what they put in the sauce or how they cooked the meat. I'll come home and find the right substitutes that work just as well. I can just see a dish and recreate it. If you don't believe me, ask anyone I've ever served a meal to.

That's what a gift is. It's something you are just a natural at. Sure, you can train up and still get better. You may still need classes to become a true expert, but the root skills were always there. Some people have it, most people don't, but you definitely do. That's your gift.

Most of us know what our gift is, we just don't know how to use it properly. For instance, I've always done 99% of the cooking in my house because there's no one else in the household with that same gift. My wife isn't fond of the kitchen, and I could always whip something nice up, no matter how little time was available.

That dynamic was in place for years before I realized that this arrangement was a sign of a gift, not just a part of my family reality.

Now, as opposed to your first two sets of streams, you may never have made a cent off of your gift. That's why you—like me—may have rarely ever thought of them at all. They were so close to you, they were just a part of you. And yet, when we pull ourselves away and get a little distance, we can see clearly that there is immense opportunity here.

That opportunity can manifest in different ways. Even though it has rarely made me money, my life has made room for my gift. That's a fact that bears repeating: Your life will make room for your gift. In my case, my gift hasn't made me income, but it has always saved me money and allowed me to create nourishing, filling, and fulfilling dishes for myself, my friends, and my family. I don't have to waste money going out to restaurants very often. I can have that experience right at home.

That doesn't mean you can't make money from your gift streams. Even now, in my own life, new, profitable streams have begun to take shape. My gift is continuing to blossom further and open up the potential for restaurant ownership and catering opportunities.

Put in the language of our streams, then, my three southern streams now look like this:

1. Cooking for my family

2. Purchasing a restaurant

3. Catering events

While all three are not currently flowing, the space is opening up in my life for them all to flow in their time.

Modeling Your Streams in the South

You may be a dreadful cook, but that's okay. That's just not your gift. Gifts can manifest anywhere in your life. You may be particularly good at listening to others, and so many people bring their problems to you so you can solve them. That's your gift. You may also be an amazing speaker. You just start talking and everyone listens. They all want to hear your stories.

Maybe, instead, you have always been able to draw. No classes needed, you could sketch someone's face or paint the sunset, so long as you had the supplies at hand. Or, perhaps it was photography, where the angles and the lighting just always made sense. Perhaps you have a true green thumb and everything you plant flourishes. Finding that gift, or rather, allowing it to step into prominence will open the space for you to transform your gift into your streams of income and fulfillment.

The trick to these three streams, then, is just identifying your gift as your gift. If you've always been good at gardening, for instance, and you can now recognize this as your gift, you may start seeing plenty of opportunities, such as:

1. Selling flowers and bouquets

2. Selling produce at a farmer's market

3. Saving money growing your own fruits, vegetables, spices, and herbs

Likewise, someone with a gift for photography may develop these streams:

1. Offering your services as an event photographer

2. Taking photos for your local newspaper

3. Becoming a portrait photographer for families or businesses

As with our other streams above, you can easily begin to see how these gifts can blossom in new and potentially lucrative directions.

A word of warning, though. Crucially, your gift has to be kept within its limits. A lot of times, we try to make our gift everything. Just like our passion, we think that we should take this one area of our life and make it our passion, our income, and our gift all in one. We want to put all our pressure of survival and flourishing onto this single skill. And, just like our passion, this can destroy our gift and remove the joy of it from our lives. David did not spend his every moment as a soldier. He was a soldier when it was time to be a soldier. I'm a cook when it's time to be a cook. My streams will flow in their right time. I'm not abandoning everything to try to become a chef just because I have that capacity. That could ruin all the joy my gift gives me.

God has given us more than just a gift. He's given us the ability to use our gift in its appropriate place. That may mean it is a gift just for us, our family, and our friends. That has been what cooking has been for me. It may just be a little extra income on the side, as you might find as a photographer. Or, it may make your fortune. The important thing is to let the streams flow as they do naturally and not to dam up your other streams and try to live solely on this set.

Filling Your Time with Flowing Streams

We can now begin to see how these streams reshape our lives. Instead of looking at life as a binary "work versus rest" relationship, we can start filling in our hours with activities that enrich our lives and enrich our pockets. We take the pressure of income off what we love and we take the need for fulfillment off our work.

Thus, our time becomes more precious, both in how we enjoy it and how it provides for us. During the day, I make a living for my family through real estate. On the weekend, I travel, doing network marketing. In the evenings and on holidays, I'm cooking. In free moments, I'm looking for a good restaurant investment opportunity. On those busy, hectic days doing real estate, I get excited by developing a dish in my mind that I'll cook that evening. When money is tight in real estate, I know more will come from network marketing and more can be saved using my kitchen.

I thus have plenty to do, plenty of ways to make money and save, and plenty of ways to find happiness in every day. And that's before we even get to our final three streams.

You, too, have been gifted with this potential. You may have overlooked it. You may never have even thought to make something of these parts of your life. Don't worry. You don't have to know what your gift is at this moment. You just need to be looking. In its time, you'll recognize it within yourself. All you have to do is seize it and use it for your income and your fulfillment.

Fill in your three streams of the South.

1.

_____

2.

_____

3.

_____

CHAPTER 17

Your Streams to the West:
Your Purpose

As we approach our final set of streams, we can look in three directions already and see a vast number of potential ways to increase our income using what we are good at, what we love to do, and what we have a natural talent for. Using these three directions and expanding those into three different income streams each provides us with far more resources to ensure we are always producing. Even as one stream may dry up temporarily, another will flood, increasing our earnings overall.

Once we've discovered these streams and opened our lives to their potential, we can worry less about work, less about money, and find more time to do what makes us happy and fulfilled.

At this point, you may wonder what else we could possibly add to our streams that might provide us with more potential for income and fulfillment. It may seem like we've maxed out all we have within us that we can translate into earning, saving, and fulfilling potential.

However, there's still one direction left, and as we stare out over the horizon to the setting sun, we can see the most important set of streams flowing toward us: our purpose.

Our purpose is distinct from the other three categories. We all know our purpose probably isn't our job. However, our purpose also isn't what we love to do, or our gift. I may be a gifted cook, but my purpose isn't to cook. A purpose goes beyond what we enjoy or what we're good at. Our purpose comes from something higher.

Unlike the other three categories, your purpose is more outward than inward. This one isn't really about you. That doesn't mean it won't be a boon to your life, your income, and your sense of fulfillment; it certainly will be. The point of it, though, is to move beyond yourself and extend the gift of these streams to others around us.

David's Purpose

Consider David's purpose. We get this right at the beginning of 1 Samuel 16, in verse one. This is the very first verse about David. To show you his purpose, let's look at the verse in full:

And the Lord said unto Samuel, How long wilt thou mourn
for Saul, seeing I have rejected him from reigning over Israel?
Fill thine horn with oil, and go, I will send thee to Jesse the
Bethlehemite: for I have provided me a king among his sons.

Right up front, God shows us that David's purpose wasn't to spend his days in the hills with the sheep. It wasn't to fight wars or to play music. Instead, from the very beginning, we learn that his purpose was to be king.

Even today, we know David best by his purpose. What comes to mind when I ask you "Who is David?" A king, that's what. It's the first fact we learn about him in the Bible, in church, in Bible study. No matter how you first encounter the man, the first fact is always the same: this man was a king. The other aspects are important to his character, but David is, above all else, a king. That was his purpose. It was there from the beginning of his existence. It was put in place by God to be discovered in a timely manner. David didn't see it at first. He didn't dream of being king while he tended to his sheep, nor even when he was soothing Saul with his music. He didn't even think of it as a great military leader when he was fighting for his life. David wasn't in charge of his purpose. God was. God knew; Samuel knew through God. David had to be told.

That's how purpose works. It comes in a revelation. It was always there, but it isn't something you choose. It's something you *discover*.

The Struggle for Our Purpose

So, what is your purpose?

Don't worry if you're struggling to understand this and come up with an answer right now. It took years for me to get my mind around this idea and to find the answer for myself. Well after I'd received the revelation of the 12 Streams of Income and Fulfillment, I was unable to fill in the final three streams for myself. I looked at my life, and I could see the first nine streams in my everyday abilities and preferences. I know I'm good a real estate. It's not what I want to do; it's what I must do. Going through trouble, I found what I like to do. I always had my gift, and for a time, I thought that might be my purpose, but I was wrong there, too. It was only when I realized that David's purpose wasn't really about *him*, it was about *his people* that I began to see my way to my purpose. David's purpose, like all of our purpose, is about God reaching out into the world through us.

That's why these last three streams are always the toughest to define. Often, someone has to show it to us. Otherwise, it has to come in a moment of clarity, a moment of revelation. We stumble into it or trip over it. It's shouted at us on the street or revealed in a random set of words we read in the newspaper. There's no way to force an answer to this one. It isn't something you can think through because it isn't something that wholly belongs to you. It has to be revealed.

Why is this so hard? Why can't we just see it and know it like the other streams? It's because your purpose often runs counter to what you know of yourself and what others know of you. Your purpose works this way because it better shows the glory of God. God places a surprising purpose within us to show His power, His will, and His glory.

David was a nobody-shepherd in the hills in Israel. No one could see his true purpose: not his father, not brothers, not his ruler, and not himself. What a powerful sign of God's glory that this nobody shepherd's purpose was to be the greatest king in history.

My Streams in the West

Likewise, no one would have guessed my purpose before the moment it was revealed. No one would have thought the boy who hated reading and hid from answering his teacher's questions would be, in the end, an author. But that's precisely what my purpose is.

Until the moment my purpose became clear, I never would have thought that God wanted to use me to write words read by the world. No one in my life saw this coming. My grandmother, who knew me best, who raised me from birth, didn't see it. My wife and my children never saw it. My friends, even my pastor, never saw it. That's what makes it such a miracle. And that's the whole point.

This book came directly from the Throne of Grace. It had to. I'm not wise enough for this. This is beyond my capability of thinking. This is beyond my natural skillset. When He gave it to me, I had no idea about streams or how to write about purpose and meaning in life. That's how your purpose will appear. It isn't something you naturally love or are naturally good at. It has to come from Him. If you grasp it, if you allow Him to work for you, it will open up these three streams and allow them to flow into your life.

And, once again, we are talking about three streams here. Just because this is my first book, it doesn't mean it's my last. Already, as I draw near the end of this first book, I have begun the next two:

1. Writing this book

2. Writing a book about health

3. Writing a book about spirituality

Now that they have been unlocked, these streams will continue to produce and flow in my life for the rest of my life. They were the last to flow, but they will flow the most fully. The income in these streams may or may not be significant. However, that's less important in these streams because it's here, in particular, that we find our full sense of fulfillment. You can't be fulfilled if you haven't lived your purpose. The richest man in the world will live a hollow life if he can't find his way to making his life *purposeful*.

So, be faithful, be watchful, and be prayerful. These streams may be hidden at this moment, but they are there. The reason you know they're there is because they are in you. Have you ever thought, "I'm supposed to do more than just *this* with my life" or "I was meant for more than *this*"? That was your purpose talking to you. That was God making His will known. You're restless and unfulfilled not because of your job or because you don't have the house you want. You're unfulfilled because you haven't let the streams of purpose flow into your life.

The good news is, those streams are still there. They may be backed up right now, but they want to flow, they want to gush, they want to flood into your life. They may not be obvious at this moment, but they are simply awaiting the right moment to make themselves known. And when will that moment be? When you have implemented the other streams, of course. Once you've made way for everything in your life in its right place, your purpose can announce itself.

These streams are an expression of you, and of God, seeking a way to come alive. By reading this book, you're giving them energy to come alive. Now, follow the advice in this book and find your other streams. Then they can flow forth.

Fill in your three streams of the West.

1.

_____

2.

_____

3.

_____

CHAPTER 18

How to Let Your Success Flow

As we bring this book to a close, I want you to take one last moment to look all around at the beautiful, powerful, potential-filled streams flowing around you. In every direction, you can now see new opportunities. These opportunities require far less effort than many life changes because they rely on what is already within you. They build on what you're good at, what you love to do, what you have a natural talent for, and what your life's purpose is. You don't have to force yourself to fit into a career anymore. You don't have to uproot your life, quit your job, and risk everything to pursue a dream anymore. You can have it all—supreme income and complete fulfillment. All it takes is being true to yourself, who you are, where you came from, and what you are meant to do.

Before I leave you, I want to address how these streams work briefly. It may seem, in your enthusiasm, that each of these streams will be flooding at every moment, and you have to pursue all of them equally and all at once.

That isn't how the streams work. While it's certainly possible that all your streams will continuously flow at the same pace, and it's likely many will all flow together at times, not every stream has to flow at every moment. Sometimes, you'll find your income comes almost exclusively from your

Streams in the East, where your work is. Sometimes, fulfillment will come just from quietly enjoying and sharing your gift in the South. At other times, your job may grow quiet while your passion in the North begins to produce for you, or the savings from your weekend pursuits with your purpose in the West get you through a season of struggle.

You have twelve streams so that you can always enjoy comfort and success while the various parts of your life go along their natural path.

It's equally important to realize that not every stream has to provide a huge income. All your streams are *capable* of producing income, but income isn't the only thing that matters in life. Perhaps your passion for music will lead to you volunteering your time, playing music for good causes. That is a wonderful way to pursue that stream. Your purpose may involve volunteering for Habitat for Humanity and helping to build shelters for those in need. You could also use that purpose to work in construction and make money, or to do your own repairs and save money, but one of those streams may simply be helping others.

Your purpose may call you to found a charity that may never earn you a dime. That is fine, and it's perfectly in line with the revelation of the 12 streams. The beauty of the 12 Streams of Income and Fulfillment is that income should no longer be a concern for you. You can feel free to invest your time and money into a charity because you have so many other streams that can deliver your financial security and advancement. Your job may end up paying you enough to get by on. Your gift may make your fortune. That would allow you plenty of room in your life to explore your purpose, which will bring you your fulfillment.

Likewise, just because your job is currently the big producer in your life, that doesn't mean it will be forever. There may come a time when you can almost shut down those streams because the others are producing so much.

Once again, look at David. He wasn't a shepherd his whole life. Shepherding was his job, and it paid the bills while he developed in other areas, but he didn't end his life a shepherd. He ended his life a king. Your life should flow in the same way. If you allow all your streams to move, some will become more dominate. Don't push against that. God is working through your streams, and if He wants you to move more into your passion or into your purpose, that's where you should go.

David ended a king, but he was also a shepherd of his people. Likewise, you may be a secretary now and may end up an organizer for your church or for a charity. You would still be doing your "job", even as that job is transformed into something new.

So, don't spend too much time trying to control the flow of each stream. As with everything in life, they will flow forth in the right season. If you are pursuing all twelve streams, you will always have money flowing toward you in one direction or another. And with so many streams to tend to, there is plenty of room to focus more on what truly matters: love, faith, family, and community.

This is crucial because these are not just streams of income, they are streams of fulfillment. And that fulfillment is your personal fulfillment as well as the fulfillment of your purpose on this earth. None of us were put here to be selfish. We are here to thrive, but we are equally here to share that thriving with others. Once we're blessed, God calls on us to share that blessing.

The real joy in my life is giving. I'm not saying there isn't value in receiving. I've needed help at times and been grateful for it. But the great joy of my life has been helping others, whether it's been giving them a hand up, a word of advice, or something more substantial. Finding my 12 Streams of Income and Fulfillment has put me in the position to be a giver, to experience that joy all the time.

This book is the culmination of my search for my own streams. It also allows my streams to flow forth and for me to use that abundance to help others and to put them in that same position.

It's true that money isn't everything. Don't let anyone tell you that life is only about getting rich. It isn't. But, at the same time, don't let anybody fool you into thinking money doesn't matter at all. Money matters in our personal lives when it gives us peace of mind. It also allows us to protect and comfort ourselves and our loved ones.

Money also gives us the ability to help others in far more effective way. With money, we're in a position to give far more of ourselves in support of our family, our friends, and our communities.

I've had money in my life, and I've been broke. You can take it from me, having money is better. There's no shame in having no money, but money makes it possible to do so much more.

The reason this book is about income and fulfillment is because they go together. You need income to pursue fulfillment. You need fulfillment for income to mean anything. Ultimately, your twelve streams do more than get you a nice house and make you feel good. They lead you to the most valuable thing in life: true, spiritual fulfillment.

Finally Discovering Your Full Potential

This book is for anyone who hasn't yet discovered their full potential. Anyone who knows they have streams within them but who finds them dammed up by their own inability to see what they should be doing in life.

What we've done in this book is recognize that the mistakes, failings, faults, and difficulties of the past were not there to kill you. They weren't there to block your way to success. They were there to make you strong and to open your life up to this very moment: the moment when all you are capable of became clear.

You are capable of success at work. You are capable of making something substantial from your passion. You were born with a gift, and you are capable of sharing and using it for your own betterment.

You have a purpose in life. And God has a purpose for you.

No mistake in the past discounts any of that. No wrong turn closes the path to your streams. They're still there, flowing and waiting for you to come to them.

The story of David teaches us that we are all kings and queens. Even the lowest among us have what it takes to be the king or queen of their own life.

Whether you've been brought low by life or you simply feel you were born to do more with your time on this planet, the same 12 Streams of Income and Fulfillment are there for you. If you follow the path I've laid out for you in this book, you can make peace with the past and use the strength and wisdom it has provided you to open the door to living in the present while pursuing your best future.

Just follow the advice, and I'll soon be seeing you in the valley of the Streams of Income and Fulfillment.

Summarize what you have learned in this book about yourself, your life and history, and God's plan for you.

Write a plan for yourself for how you will begin to move toward your 12 Streams of Income and Fulfillment TODAY. Start with the very first thing you can do to move in the right direction and consider all the major steps from there.

_____

_____

_____

_____

_____

_____

_____